D1433933

Blazing Barbecue

Blazing
Barbecue

101 recipes for brilliant barbecues

This edition published in 2013
LOVE FOOD is an imprint of Parragon Books Ltd

Parragon
Chartist House
15–17 Trim Street
Bath, BA1 1HA, UK

Copyright © Parragon Books Ltd 2007

LOVE FOOD and the accompanying heart device is a registered trade mark of Parragon
Books Ltd in Australia, the UK, USA, India and the EU.

www.parragon.com/lovefood

All rights reserved. No part of this publication may be reproduced, stored in
aretrieval system or transmitted, in any form or by any means, electronic, mechanical,
photocopying, recording or otherwise, without the prior permission of the copyright
holder.

ISBN: 978-1-4723-0348-6

Printed in China

Photography by Günter Beer
Home Economist Stevan Paul
Internal design by Talking Design
Introduction by Anna Brandenburger

Notes for the Reader
This book uses both metric and imperial measurements. Follow the same units of
measurement throughout; do not mix metric and imperial. All spoon measurements are
level: teaspoons are assumed to be 5 ml, and tablespoons are assumed to be 15 ml.
Unless otherwise stated, milk is assumed to be full fat, eggs and individual vegetables
are medium, and pepper is freshly ground black pepper. Unless otherwise stated, all root
vegetables should be washed in plain water and peeled prior to using.

For best results, use a food thermometer when cooking meat and poultry – check the
latest government guidelines for current advice.

Garnishes, decorations and serving suggestions are all optional and not necessarily
included in the recipe ingredients or method.

The times given are an approximate guide only. Preparation times differ according to
the techniques used by different people and the cooking times may also vary from those
given. Optional ingredients, variations or serving suggestions have not been included in
the time calculations.

Recipes using raw or very lightly cooked eggs should be avoided by infants, the elderly,
pregnant women, convalescents and anyone suffering from an illness. Pregnant and
breastfeeding women are advised to avoid eating peanuts and peanut products.
Sufferers from nut allergies should be aware that some of the ready-made ingredients
used in the recipes in this book may contain nuts. Always check the packaging before use.

CONTENTS

Introduction

You know summer has arrived when the familiar smell of charcoal smoke starts wafting over back garden fences. As the gloom of cold wet winter days disappears and the sun gains its strength, our natural inclination is to spend as much time outdoors as possible. Cooking and entertaining with a barbecue is the obvious choice when it is either too warm to fire up the indoor oven or you simply want to be able to spend more time socialising while cooking.

Simple food – and lots of it – is the best: even plain sausages are totally transformed on a barbecue with a smoky, crisp barbecued skin. An important point to remember is that everything tastes better in the fresh air and the delicious cooking smells only add to the hunger level, which means that everyone's appetite somehow increases when eating outside.

Barbecues need not be limited just to the back garden or patio; you can easily take a portable or disposable barbecue along on your camping trip, picnic on the beach or even up a mountain. With just a little forward planning you can easily cook up a feast wherever you choose.

As well as the actual barbecued food, do not forget all the extras. In this book there is a wealth of sumptuous salads, sauces and wonderful desserts that all add to the occasion. Try some of the cocktails – both alcoholic and non-alcoholic – guaranteed to get the party started.

Getting Started

Choosing a barbecue

There are so many different sorts of barbecues on the market that it is often a daunting task to know where to begin. You can find everything from the disposable filled foil tray in supermarkets and garage forecourts, all the way up to the extremely sophisticated gas barbecues that light at the flick of a switch and come with masses of gadgets and dials. A good way to start your search is to think about how and when you are likely to use the barbecue. If you live in an area where you know the weather is only likely to afford you a few warm weekends, do not think too big. If, on the other hand, you have a large family or enjoy entertaining, a small kettle barbecue will definitely not suffice, and it might even be worth building your own brick barbecue.

One of the first choices to make is whether you want to use gas or charcoal for heat. This is more of a lifestyle choice. If you are convinced that food cooked over hot charcoal has the best flavour and take pride in getting the fire started, then charcoal is for you. Alternatively, if you want the perfect fire at the touch of a button and to be able to control the temperature, then a gas barbecue is the ideal choice.

Charcoal barbecues

The **kettle barbecue** comes with a lid which is great for cooking larger pieces of meat, or even whole birds, by keeping in the heat. It also means that if the rain decides to start at just the wrong time, you can continue cooking. These are sturdy pieces of equipment that often come with wheels for easy mobility.

Flat-bed barbecues often have a larger area for cooking and sometimes come with varying levels on which to fit the grill racks. This is useful when cooking a large amount of food as you can move food that is nearly cooked up to a higher rack.

Brick or masonry **built-in barbecues** are great if you have a large garden and really enjoy barbecuing on a regular basis. They can be built to your own simple design using household bricks and a sturdy metal tray and rack. Alternatively, there are many ready-built or DIY kits available.

Portable charcoal barbecues come in a variety of shapes and are usually made to fold closed for easy carrying. They also usually come with legs to attach while cooking so the hot base is not directly on the ground.

Disposable barbecues cost just a few pounds from supermarkets and garages. They are perfect for picnics or the occasional back garden barbecue. They are very easy to use and heat up in a matter of minutes, although they do not stay hot for very long so are really only good for food that cooks quickly. They come in various sizes depending on how much food you have to cook. They are also good for keeping vegetarian food separate.

Gas barbecues

Gas barbecues run from the basic barbecue with an area below to store the gas cylinder, all the way up to a huge 6-burner mega-contraption with pan hot plates on one side, a rotisserie area and warming ovens. They all have covers that easily lift and lower and come with wheels so you can position them where you like. The choice is really down to the size of your budget.

Portable gas barbecues offer the easiest way to cook up a great meal while out and about. They are neat and compact, if a little heavy, and have all the speed and convenience of their larger cousins.

Fuel types

Charcoal briquettes are the most common type of fuel for charcoal barbecues. They are often made from sawdust, wood scraps and binders with chemicals added to enhance burning. Some briquettes are impregnated with a lighting agent and sold in bags as **instant lighting charcoal**. These bags are placed directly into the barbecue and the bag itself is lit.

Hardwood charcoals are natural additive-free wood chunks that have been carbonised in an oxygen-free oven. The advantage of these is that they burn cleanly and somewhat hotter than the briquettes, but they sometimes give out sparks at first.

Woodchips for barbecues are generally made from hardwood and their aroma is wonderful, but they can be difficult to get started. They can lose their heat sooner than charcoal so are suitable when cooking small amounts of food. Some woodchips are 'flavoured' with hickory or mesquite which gives the food a delicious flavour. If the chips are first soaked for 30 to 60 minutes in water, they will gently smoke rather than catch light.

Barbecuing food directly over just **wood** is a little more difficult. This is because the wood burns fiercely for a shorter time and then cools rapidly. If you do choose this fuel, however, opt for apple, oak or cherry and avoid pine as it exudes noxious smoke that will ruin the food.

Gas barbecues take **propane** or **butane gas** in various sizes of bottles and cylinders. They generally fit underneath the grill area and have secure valves to shut off the gas supply once you have finished cooking. Always store gas cylinders or bottles outside and protect them from direct sunlight and frost. It is not advisable to keep more spare cylinders than you need. The bottles and cylinders can be ordered from gas suppliers who will deliver them or they can be bought from large homeware shops.

Tips for getting started

Lighting a charcoal barbecue is not difficult, but there are a few general rules to follow. Firstly, keep the charcoal briquettes dry, preferably in an airtight container, to help the charcoal light faster. Place the briquettes in a pyramid in the centre of the barbecue. If you are using barbecue lighter fluid, douse this evenly over the briquettes and allow to soak in for a few minutes. If using barbecue fire lighters, poke these between the briquettes about a third of the way up the pyramid. Using long kitchen matches, either light the doused briquettes or the fire lighters. The charcoal will take about 30 minutes to get hot. Once the briquettes start to get hot, they will glow a red to orange colour, then gradually turn a whitish grey. It is the white ash over the coals that tells you they are really hot. Now you can spread them out evenly over the bottom of the barbecue. Do not worry if some of the coals from the centre of the pyramid are still orange – just give them a few more minutes to turn grey too. Place the grill rack over the top. It is a good idea to wait a few minutes before adding the food, in order to allow the rack to heat up.

If you are cooking over wood, a similar principal applies as to charcoal. These fires start up best by using barbecue fire lighters tucked in between the pieces of wood. Again, light the blocks of wood in a pyramid and when they are burning well, and the flames have subsided somewhat, spread them out to an even layer and place the metal rack on top.

Gas barbecues are the easiest of all to light. Depending on your model there are a variety of controls (refer to your manufacturer's guidelines). It is usually best to light the barbecue to its hottest setting and then reduce the heat as needed. First open the barbecue lid, then the gas tank. Allow 2 to 3 seconds for the gas chamber to fill, then push the ignite button. Once all the burners are lit, close the lid to allow it to preheat. When hot, place the food on the grill and adjust the burners to the desired heat.

Useful equipment

There are masses of barbecue gadgets on the market, but only a few of these are really necessary:

Tongs are probably the most important tool you will need, so it is important to have a good sturdy pair that will grasp the food well and save you from burning your fingers.

Oven gloves are a good idea if you have a large barbecue and have to reach over the hot coals.

Basting brushes allow you to marinate your food, adding flavour and moisture, as it cooks.

Wooden or metal skewers are a good idea when barbecuing smaller items. If you choose wooden skewers, make sure that you soak them in water for at least 30 minutes before using so they do not catch light.

Hinged wire racks make cooking less stable items, such as fish or home-made burgers, much easier. Smaller items can be cooked together and turned all at the same time which allows for more even cooking.

Meat thermometers are essential if you are cooking a large piece of meat as it can be difficult to judge whether it is cooked through.

Long handled spatulas are great for turning food and removing it once cooked.

An **oil spray** can be used to spray the grill rack or flat plate before cooking to prevent the food from sticking.

A **wire brush** is useful for removing any burnt-on debris from the grill rack during and after use. For best results, clean while the rack is still warm.

Fire and food safety

Once you have decided which type of barbecue to buy, the next step is to choose the site. It is crucial that the barbecue is placed on level ground where it cannot wobble or tip over – this makes cooking easier as well as safer. For fire safety, make sure the barbecue is a good distance from any houses, sheds, fences or overhanging trees. A sheltered position will help the barbecue heat up more evenly and cut down on smoke blowing about. Keep a bucket of water or a fire blanket nearby and never leave a hot barbecue unattended.

Once the barbecue has done its work, allow it to cool completely. With charcoal barbecues, the cool ash can be disposed of by tipping it on to bare garden soil or into a plastic bag and then into the rubbish bin.

For a healthy barbecue, there are a few points to remember about food storage, preparation and cooking:
• All frozen food must be completely defrosted before cooking.
• Store uncooked meat, poultry and fish in airtight containers in the refrigerator until needed. For a large party or picnic, invest in a cool box. It is best to return raw foods to room temperature for about 1 hour before cooking.
• Use different chopping boards and utensils for raw and cooked foods.
• Do not put raw and nearly-cooked meat next to each other on the grill.
• Poultry should be cooked thoroughly so that no pink remains.
• Do not crowd the grill – allow a few centimetres between items.
• If the marinade you are using for basting has been in contact with uncooked meat, poultry or seafood, make sure that you do not use it during the last few minutes of cooking otherwise any harmful bacteria may not be destroyed by the heat of the barbecue. The safest way is to reserve a portion of the marinade for basting before adding raw foods.

Tips for the perfect barbecue party

Gathering around the garden barbecue is not usually a formal occasion. However, a certain amount of careful planning and smartening up of the garden or patio will create the perfect party atmosphere and ensure that everything runs smoothly.

Here are some ideas to help:

- Have plenty of disposable plates, glasses and cutlery on hand. Even if you plan to use your usual crockery and cutlery, they are always useful for extra guests or small children.
- Serve crisps and snacks in bowls placed around the garden or patio so guests are happy to spread out and do not all hover in one area.
- Find a good spot to place a large tub of ice, and fill it with bottles and cans of drink. Guests will be able to help themselves to drinks, saving you the job of re-filling everyone's glasses. Remember the bottle openers and corkscrews!
- Provide a good supply of non-alcoholic drinks. If the party is running for quite a few hours on a hot afternoon, people are going to drink quite a lot and will not want just alcoholic drinks.
- See if you can find or borrow outdoor games for children of all ages to keep them occupied and happy.

- Appetites are always enhanced when eating outdoors so plan on larger portions than usual.
- Aim for two or three different main course choices and have lots of salads and bread on hand so people can help themselves.
- Make sure you have enough non-meat items for any vegetarian guests.
- If you are entertaining a crowd and think your barbecue might not be big enough to cook all the food at once, you can pre-cook some in the oven. Then re-heat it on the barbecue to give it that wonderful smoky flavour and crispy skin; just make sure it is piping hot all the way through.

Countdown to a barbecue party:

1 week ahead
- If you have a gas barbecue, check that the gas cylinder is full and the valves are in good working order. If your cylinder is less than half full, order a full one to use for the party. With a charcoal barbecue, make sure that you have enough charcoal and lighting agent.
- Rent or borrow glasses if necessary.
- Count up guest numbers and chase up any guests who have not responded.
- Find out if any of your guests have special dietary requirements and plan what you are going to cook.
- Shop for non-perishable items, such as drinks, crisps, sauces and relishes. Remember to stock up on rubbish bags!
- Check that outdoor furniture is in good condition and you have enough chairs, table cloths, napkins and serving platters. If it is an evening party, shop for candles, garden lanterns and insect repellent.

1 day ahead
- Shop for meat, poultry, fish, fresh fruit and vegetables.
- Marinate meat, poultry or fish, as well as vegetables, and prepare side dishes and sauces. Start to prepare any puddings that can be made ahead and stored.
- Clear space in the refrigerator for drinks and salads.
- Have a last minute tidy up around the garden and make sure your flowers and lawn are well watered. Sweep and clean up patio or deck areas.
- Check weather forecasts and make indoor plans if there is a good chance of rain. If weather permits, set up chairs and tables outside.

On the day
- Buy ice and place in a large container to keep drinks cool and free up fridge space.
- Prepare salads (do not add dressing until serving) and put finishing touches to side dishes and desserts.

1 hour ahead
- Prepare the barbecue for lighting.
- Remove marinated food from the refrigerator to allow it to come up to room temperature.

Barbecue Classics

boozy beef steaks

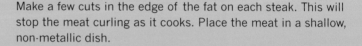

serves 4

4 beef steaks
4 tbsp whisky or brandy
2 tbsp soy sauce
1 tbsp dark muscovado
   sugar
pepper
tomato slices
fresh parsley sprigs,
   to garnish
garlic bread, to serve

Make a few cuts in the edge of the fat on each steak. This will stop the meat curling as it cooks. Place the meat in a shallow, non-metallic dish.

Mix the whisky, soy sauce, sugar and pepper to taste together in a small bowl, stirring until the sugar dissolves. Pour the mixture over the steak. Cover with clingfilm and leave to marinate in the refrigerator for at least 2 hours.

Preheat the barbecue. Cook the meat over hot coals, searing the meat over the hottest part of the barbecue for 2 minutes on each side.

Move the meat to an area with slightly less intense heat and cook for a further 4–10 minutes on each side, depending on how well done you like your steaks. To test if the meat is cooked, insert the point of a sharp knife into the meat – the juices will run from red when the meat is still rare, to clear as it becomes well cooked.

Lightly barbecue the tomato slices for 1–2 minutes. Transfer the meat and the tomatoes to warmed serving plates. Garnish with fresh parsley sprigs and serve with garlic bread.

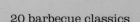

a sizzling dish with a touch of spice

barbecued steak fajitas

serves 4

2 tbsp sunflower oil,
 plus extra for oiling
finely grated rind of 1 lime
1 tbsp lime juice
2 garlic cloves, crushed
¼ tsp ground coriander
¼ tsp ground cumin
pinch of sugar
salt and pepper
1 piece of rump steak,
 about 675 g/1 lb 8 oz
 and 2 cm/¾ inch thick
4 wheat tortillas
1 avocado
2 tomatoes, thinly sliced
4 tbsp soured cream
4 spring onions,
 thinly sliced

To make the marinade, put the oil, lime rind and juice, garlic, coriander, cumin, sugar and salt and pepper to taste into a large, shallow, non-metallic dish large enough to hold the steak and mix together. Add the steak and turn in the marinade to coat it. Cover and leave to marinate in the refrigerator for 6–8 hours or up to 24 hours, turning occasionally.

When ready to cook, preheat the barbecue. Using a slotted spoon, remove the steak from the marinade, put on to an oiled grill rack and cook over a medium heat for 5 minutes for rare or 8–10 minutes for medium, turning the steak frequently and basting once or twice with any remaining marinade.

Meanwhile, warm the tortillas according to the instructions on the packet. Peel and slice the avocado.

Thinly slice the steak across the grain and arrange an equal quantity of the slices on one side of each tortilla. Add the tomato and avocado slices, top with a spoonful of soured cream and sprinkle over the spring onions. Fold over and eat at once.

barbecued **pork** sausages with thyme

serves 4

1 garlic clove, finely
   chopped
1 onion, grated
1 small red chilli, deseeded
   and finely chopped
450 g/1 lb lean minced
   pork
50 g/1¾ oz almonds,
   toasted and ground
50 g/1¾ oz fresh
   breadcrumbs
1 tbsp finely chopped
   fresh thyme
salt and pepper
flour, for dusting
vegetable oil, for brushing

to serve
fresh finger rolls
slices of onion,
   lightly cooked
tomato ketchup and/
   or mustard

Put the garlic, onion, chilli, pork, almonds, breadcrumbs and fresh thyme into a large bowl. Season well with salt and pepper and mix until well combined.

Using your hands, form the mixture into sausage shapes. Roll each sausage in a little flour, then transfer to a bowl, cover with clingfilm and refrigerate for 45 minutes.

Preheat the barbecue. Brush a piece of aluminium foil with oil, then put the sausages on the foil and brush them with a little more vegetable oil. Transfer the sausages and foil to the barbecue.

Barbecue over hot coals, turning the sausages frequently, for about 15 minutes, or until cooked right through. Serve with finger rolls, cooked sliced onion and tomato ketchup and/or mustard.

these tangy ribs will disappear in minutes

spicy ribs

serves 4

1 onion, chopped
2 garlic cloves, chopped
2.5-cm/1-inch piece
   fresh root ginger, sliced
1 fresh red chilli, deseeded
   and chopped
5 tbsp dark soy sauce
3 tbsp lime juice
1 tbsp palm or muscovado
   sugar
2 tbsp groundnut oil
salt and pepper
1 kg/2 lb 4 oz pork spare
   ribs, separated

Preheat the barbecue. Put the onion, garlic, ginger, chilli and soy sauce into a food processor and process to a paste. Transfer to a jug and stir in the lime juice, sugar and oil and season to taste with salt and pepper.

Place the spare ribs in a preheated wok or large, heavy-based saucepan and pour in the soy sauce mixture. Place on the hob and bring to the boil, then simmer over a low heat, stirring frequently, for 30 minutes. If the mixture appears to be drying out, add a little water.

Remove the spare ribs, reserving the sauce. Cook the ribs over medium hot coals, turning and basting frequently with the sauce, for 20–30 minutes. Transfer to a large serving plate and serve immediately.

pork with a wonderfully messy sticky glaze

honey-glazed
pork chops

· ·

serves 4

4 lean pork loin chops
salt and pepper
4 tbsp clear honey
1 tbsp dry sherry
4 tbsp orange juice
2 tbsp olive oil
2.5-cm/1-inch piece
   fresh root ginger, grated
sunflower oil, for oiling

Preheat the barbecue. Season the pork chops with salt and pepper to taste. Reserve while you make the glaze.

To make the glaze, place the honey, sherry, orange juice, olive oil and ginger in a small saucepan and heat gently, stirring constantly, until well blended.

Cook the pork chops on an oiled rack over hot coals for 5 minutes on each side.

Brush the chops with the glaze and barbecue for a further 2–4 minutes on each side, basting frequently with the glaze.

Transfer the pork chops to warmed serving plates and serve hot.

the spicy marinade gives lamb a whole new dimension

^{spicy} lamb steaks

serves 4

4 lamb steaks, about
  175 g/6 oz each
8 fresh rosemary sprigs
8 fresh bay leaves
2 tbsp olive oil

spicy marinade
2 tbsp sunflower oil
1 large onion,
  finely chopped
2 garlic cloves,
  finely chopped
2 tbsp jerk seasoning
1 tbsp curry paste
1 tsp grated fresh root
  ginger
400 g/14 oz canned
  chopped tomatoes
4 tbsp Worcestershire
  sauce
3 tbsp light muscovado
  sugar
salt and pepper

To make the marinade, heat the oil in a heavy-based saucepan. Add the onion and garlic and cook, stirring occasionally, for 5 minutes, or until softened. Stir in the jerk seasoning, curry paste and grated ginger and cook, stirring constantly, for 2 minutes. Add the tomatoes, Worcestershire sauce and sugar, then season to taste with salt and pepper. Bring to the boil, stirring constantly, then reduce the heat and simmer for 15 minutes, or until thickened. Remove from the heat and leave to cool.

Place the lamb steaks between 2 sheets of clingfilm and beat with the side of a rolling pin to flatten. Transfer the steaks to a large, shallow, non-metallic dish. Pour the marinade over them, turning to coat. Cover with clingfilm and leave to marinate in the refrigerator for 3 hours.

Preheat the barbecue. Drain the lamb, reserving the marinade. Cook the lamb over medium hot coals, brushing frequently with the marinade, for 5–7 minutes on each side. Meanwhile, dip the rosemary and bay leaves in the olive oil and cook on the barbecue for 3–5 minutes. Serve the lamb immediately with the herbs.

minted lamb chops

serves 6

6 chump chops, about
   175 g/6 oz each
150 ml/5 fl oz natural
   Greek yogurt
2 garlic cloves, finely
   chopped
1 tsp grated fresh root
   ginger
¼ tsp coriander seeds,
   crushed
salt and pepper
1 tbsp olive oil, plus extra
   for brushing
1 tbsp orange juice
1 tsp walnut oil
2 tbsp chopped fresh mint

Place the chops in a large, shallow, non-metallic bowl. Mix half the yogurt, the garlic, ginger and coriander seeds together in a jug and season to taste with salt and pepper. Spoon the mixture over the chops, turning to coat, then cover with clingfilm and leave to marinate in the refrigerator for 2 hours, turning occasionally.

Preheat the barbecue. Place the remaining yogurt, the olive oil, orange juice, walnut oil and mint in a small bowl and, using a hand-held blender, mix until thoroughly blended. Season to taste with salt and pepper. Cover the minted yogurt with clingfilm and leave to chill in the refrigerator until ready to serve.

Drain the chops, scraping off the marinade. Brush with olive oil and cook over medium hot coals for 5–7 minutes on each side. Serve immediately with the minted yogurt.

this barbecue favourite is sure
to be a hit

cajun chicken

serves 4

4 chicken drumsticks
4 chicken thighs
2 fresh corn cobs, husks
  and silks removed
85 g/3 oz butter, melted

spice mix
2 tsp onion powder
2 tsp paprika
1½ tsp salt
1 tsp garlic powder
1 tsp dried thyme
1 tsp cayenne pepper
1 tsp ground black pepper
½ tsp ground white pepper
¼ tsp ground cumin

Preheat the barbecue. Using a sharp knife, make 2–3 diagonal slashes in the chicken drumsticks and thighs, then place them in a large dish. Cut the corn cobs into thick slices and add them to the dish. Mix all the ingredients for the spice mix together in a small bowl.

Brush the chicken and corn with the melted butter and sprinkle with the spice mix. Toss to coat well.

Cook the chicken over medium hot coals, turning occasionally, for 15 minutes, then add the corn slices and cook, turning occasionally, for a further 10–15 minutes, or until beginning to blacken slightly at the edges. Transfer to a large serving plate and serve immediately.

spicy chicken wings

serves 4

16 chicken wings
4 tbsp sunflower oil
4 tbsp light soy sauce
5-cm/2-inch piece fresh
    root ginger, roughly
    chopped
2 garlic cloves, roughly
    chopped
juice and grated rind
    of 1 lemon
2 tsp ground cinnamon
2 tsp ground turmeric
4 tbsp clear honey
salt and pepper

sauce

2 orange peppers
2 yellow peppers
sunflower oil,
    for brushing
125 ml/4 fl oz natural
    yogurt
2 tbsp dark soy sauce
2 tbsp chopped fresh
    coriander

Place the chicken wings in a large, shallow, non-metallic dish. Put the oil, soy sauce, ginger, garlic, lemon rind and juice, cinnamon, turmeric and honey into a food processor and process to a smooth purée. Season to taste with salt and pepper. Spoon the mixture over the chicken wings and turn until thoroughly coated, cover with clingfilm and leave to marinate in the refrigerator for up to 8 hours.

Preheat the barbecue. To make the sauce, brush the peppers with the oil and cook over hot coals, turning frequently, for 10 minutes, or until the skin is blackened and charred. Remove from the barbecue and leave to cool slightly, then peel off the skins and discard the seeds. Put the flesh into a food processor with the yogurt and process to a smooth purée. Transfer to a bowl and stir in the soy sauce and chopped coriander.

Drain the chicken wings, reserving the marinade. Cook over medium hot coals, turning and brushing frequently with the reserved marinade, for 8–10 minutes, or until thoroughly cooked. Serve immediately with the sauce.

perhaps one of the best-known
Caribbean dishes

jerk chicken

· ·

serves 4

4 lean chicken portions
1 bunch spring onions,
  trimmed
1–2 Scotch Bonnet chillies,
  deseeded
1 garlic clove
5-cm/2-inch piece root
  ginger, peeled and
  roughly chopped
½ tsp dried thyme
½ tsp paprika
¼ tsp ground allspice
pinch ground cinnamon
pinch ground cloves
4 tbsp white wine vinegar
3 tbsp light soy sauce
pepper

Rinse the chicken portions and pat them dry on absorbent kitchen paper. Place them in a shallow dish.

Place the spring onions, chillies, garlic, ginger, thyme, paprika, allspice, cinnamon, cloves, wine vinegar, soy sauce and pepper to taste in a food processor and process until smooth.

Pour the spicy mixture over the chicken. Turn the chicken portions over so that they are well coated in the marinade.

Transfer the chicken portions to the refrigerator and leave to marinate for up to 24 hours.

Remove the chicken from the marinade and barbecue over medium hot coals for about 30 minutes, turning the chicken over and basting occasionally with any remaining marinade, until the chicken is browned and cooked through.

Transfer the chicken portions to individual serving plates and serve at once.

chicken with a piquant sweet-and-sour glaze

mustard & honey
drumsticks

serves 4

8 chicken drumsticks
salad leaves, to serve

glaze
125 ml/4 fl oz clear honey
4 tbsp Dijon mustard
4 tbsp wholegrain
 mustard
4 tbsp white wine vinegar
2 tbsp sunflower oil
salt and pepper

Using a sharp knife, make 2–3 diagonal slashes in the chicken drumsticks and place them in a large, non-metallic dish.

Mix all the ingredients for the glaze together in a jug and season to taste with salt and pepper. Pour the glaze over the drumsticks, turning until the drumsticks are well coated. Cover with clingfilm and leave to marinate in the refrigerator for at least 1 hour.

Preheat the barbecue. Drain the chicken drumsticks, reserving the marinade. Cook the chicken over medium hot coals, turning frequently and brushing with the reserved marinade, for 25–30 minutes, or until thoroughly cooked. Transfer to serving plates and serve immediately with the salad leaves.

this wonderfully aromatic rub is perfect with fish

charred **fish**

• •

serves 4

4 white fish steaks
1 tbsp paprika
1 tsp dried thyme
1 tsp cayenne pepper
1 tsp black pepper
½ tsp white pepper
½ tsp salt
¼ tsp ground allspice
50 g/1¾ oz unsalted butter
3 tbsp sunflower oil
green beans, to serve

Preheat the barbecue. Rinse the fish steaks under cold running water and pat dry with kitchen paper.

Mix the paprika, thyme, cayenne, black and white peppers, salt and allspice together in a shallow dish.

Place the butter and sunflower oil in a small saucepan and heat gently, stirring occasionally, until the butter melts.

Brush the butter mixture liberally all over the fish steaks, on both sides, then dip the fish into the spicy mix until coated on both sides.

Cook the fish over hot coals for 3 minutes on each side until cooked through. Continue to baste the fish with the remaining butter mixture during the cooking time. Serve with the green beans.

this fruity dish is the perfect
crowd-pleaser

salmon
with mango salsa

serves 4

4 salmon steaks, about
   175 g/6 oz each
finely grated rind
   and juice of 1 lime or
   ½ lemon
salt and pepper

salsa
1 large mango, peeled,
   stoned and diced
1 red onion, finely chopped
2 passion fruit
2 fresh basil sprigs
2 tbsp lime juice
salt

Preheat the barbecue. Rinse the salmon steaks under cold
running water, pat dry with kitchen paper and place in a large,
shallow, non-metallic dish. Sprinkle with the lime rind and pour
the juice over them. Season to taste with salt and pepper, cover
and leave to stand while you make the salsa.

Place the mango flesh in a bowl with the onion. Cut the passion
fruit in half and scoop out the seeds and pulp with a teaspoon
into the bowl. Tear the basil leaves and add them to the bowl with
the lime juice. Season to taste with salt and stir well. Cover with
clingfilm and reserve until required.

Cook the salmon steaks over medium hot coals for 3–4 minutes
on each side. Serve immediately with the salsa.

chargrilled tuna with chilli salsa

serves 4

4 tuna steaks, about
  175 g/6 oz each
grated rind and juice
  of 1 lime
2 tbsp olive oil
salt and pepper
fresh coriander sprigs,
  to garnish
lettuce leaves, to garnish
crusty bread, to serve

chilli salsa
2 orange peppers
1 tbsp olive oil
juice of 1 lime
juice of 1 orange
2–3 fresh red chillies,
  deseeded and chopped
pinch of cayenne pepper

Rinse the tuna thoroughly under cold running water and pat dry with kitchen paper, then place in a large, shallow, non-metallic dish. Sprinkle with the lime rind and pour the juice and olive oil over the fish. Season to taste with salt and pepper, cover with clingfilm and leave to marinate in the refrigerator for up to 1 hour.

Preheat the barbecue. To make the salsa, brush the peppers with the olive oil and cook over hot coals, turning frequently, for 10 minutes, or until the skin is blackened and charred. Remove from the barbecue and leave to cool slightly, then peel off the skins and discard the seeds. Put the peppers into a food processor with the remaining salsa ingredients and process to a purée. Transfer to a bowl and season to taste with salt and pepper.

Cook the tuna over hot coals for 4–5 minutes on each side, until golden. Transfer to serving plates, garnish with coriander sprigs and lettuce leaves, and serve with the salsa and plenty of crusty bread.

aubergine & mozzarella
sandwiches

serves 2

1 large aubergine
1 tbsp lemon juice
3 tbsp olive oil
salt and pepper
125 g/4½ oz grated
  mozzarella cheese
2 sun-dried tomatoes,
  chopped

to serve
Italian bread
mixed salad leaves
tomato slices

Preheat the barbecue. Using a sharp knife, slice the aubergine into thin rounds.

Mix the lemon juice and olive oil together in a small bowl and season the mixture with salt and pepper to taste. Brush the aubergine slices with the olive oil and lemon juice mixture and cook over medium hot coals for 2–3 minutes, without turning, until golden on the under side.

Turn half of the aubergine slices over and sprinkle with cheese and chopped sun-dried tomatoes.

Place the remaining aubergine slices on top of the cheese and tomatoes, turning them so that the pale side is uppermost. Barbecue for 1–2 minutes, then carefully turn the whole sandwich over and barbecue for a further 1–2 minutes. Baste with the olive oil mixture.

Serve in Italian bread with mixed salad leaves and a few slices of tomato.

a delicious mix of vegetables, beans and cheese

vegetarian
sausages

serves 4

1 tbsp sunflower oil, plus extra for oiling
1 small onion, finely chopped
50 g/1¾ oz mushrooms, finely chopped
½ red pepper, deseeded and finely chopped
400 g/14 oz canned cannellini beans, rinsed and drained
100 g/3½ oz fresh breadcrumbs
100 g/3½ oz Cheddar cheese, grated
1 tsp dried mixed herbs
1 egg yolk
seasoned plain flour

to serve
small bread rolls
fried onion slices
tomato chutney

Heat the sunflower oil in a saucepan. Add the onion, mushrooms and pepper and fry until softened.

Mash the cannellini beans in a large bowl. Add the onion, mushroom and pepper mixture, the breadcrumbs, cheese, herbs and egg yolk and mix well. Press the mixture together with your fingers and shape into 8 sausages. Roll each sausage in the seasoned flour. Leave to chill in the refrigerator for at least 30 minutes.

Preheat the barbecue. Cook the sausages on a sheet of oiled foil set over medium hot coals for 15–20 minutes, turning and basting frequently with oil, until golden. Split bread rolls down the centre and insert a layer of fried onions. Place the sausages in the rolls and serve with tomato chutney.

Entertaining

earthy mushrooms complement steak perfectly

beef
with wild mushrooms

serves 4

4 beef steaks
50 g/1¾ oz butter
1–2 garlic cloves, crushed
150 g/5½ oz mixed wild
   mushrooms
2 tbsp chopped fresh
   parsley

to serve
salad leaves
cherry tomatoes, halved

Preheat the barbecue. Place the steaks on a chopping board and using a sharp knife, cut a pocket into the side of each steak.

To make the stuffing, heat the butter in a large frying pan. Add the garlic and fry gently for 1 minute. Add the mushrooms to the frying pan and sauté gently for 4–6 minutes, or until tender. Remove the frying pan from the heat and stir in the parsley.

Divide the mushroom mixture into 4 and insert a portion into the pocket of each steak. Seal the pocket with a cocktail stick. If preparing ahead, allow the mixture to cool before stuffing the steaks.

Cook the steaks over hot coals, searing the meat over the hottest part of the barbecue for 2 minutes on each side. Move the steaks to an area with slightly less intense heat and barbecue for a further 4–10 minutes on each side, depending on how well done you like your steaks.

Transfer the steaks to serving plates and remove the cocktail sticks. Serve with salad leaves and cherry tomatoes.

tabasco steaks
with watercress butter

serves 4

1 bunch of watercress
85 g/3 oz unsalted butter,
  softened
4 sirloin steaks, about
  225 g/8 oz each
4 tsp Tabasco sauce
salt and pepper

Preheat the barbecue. Using a sharp knife, finely chop enough watercress to fill 4 tablespoons. Reserve a few watercress leaves for the garnish. Place the butter in a small bowl and beat in the chopped watercress with a fork until fully incorporated. Cover with clingfilm and leave to chill in the refrigerator until required. Sprinkle each steak with 1 teaspoon of the Tabasco sauce, rubbing it in well. Season to taste with salt and pepper.

Cook the steaks over hot coals for 2½ minutes each side for rare, 4 minutes each side for medium and 6 minutes each side for well done. Transfer to serving plates, garnish with the reserved watercress leaves and serve immediately, topped with the watercress butter.

this dish brings a touch of class to any party

rack
& ruin

serves 4

4 racks of lamb, each with
   4 cutlets
2 tbsp extra-virgin olive oil
1 tbsp balsamic vinegar
1 tbsp lemon juice
3 tbsp finely chopped
   fresh rosemary
1 small onion, finely
   chopped
salt and pepper

Place the racks of lamb in a large, shallow, non-metallic dish. Place the oil, vinegar, lemon juice, rosemary and onion in a jug and stir together. Season to taste with salt and pepper.

Pour the marinade over the lamb and turn until thoroughly coated. Cover with clingfilm and leave to marinate in the refrigerator for 1 hour, turning occasionally.

Preheat the barbecue. Drain the racks of lamb, reserving the marinade. Cook over medium hot coals, brushing frequently with the marinade, for 10 minutes on each side. Serve immediately.

butterfly lamb
with balsamic vinegar & mint

serves 4

1 boned leg of lamb,
   about 1.8 kg/4 lb
8 tbsp balsamic vinegar
grated rind and juice
   of 1 lemon
150 ml/5 fl oz sunflower oil
4 tbsp chopped fresh mint
2 garlic cloves, crushed
2 tbsp light muscovado
   sugar
salt and pepper

to serve

barbecued vegetables,
   such as peppers and
   courgettes
black or green olives

Open out the boned leg of lamb so that its shape resembles a butterfly. Thread 2–3 skewers through the meat to make it easier to turn on the barbecue.

Mix the balsamic vinegar, lemon rind and juice, sunflower oil, mint, garlic, sugar and salt and pepper to taste together in a non-metallic dish that is large enough to hold the lamb. Place the lamb in the dish and turn it over a few times so that the meat is coated on both sides with the marinade. Cover and leave to marinate in the refrigerator for at least 6 hours, or preferably overnight, turning occasionally.

Preheat the barbecue. Remove the lamb from the marinade and reserve the liquid for basting. Place the rack about 15 cm/6 inches above the coals and cook the lamb for 30 minutes on each side, turning once and basting frequently with the marinade.

Transfer the lamb to a chopping board and remove the skewers. Cut the lamb into slices across the grain and serve with barbecued vegetables and olives.

a classic combination of herb and citrus flavours

lemon & herb
pork escalopes

serves 4

4 pork escalopes
2 tbsp sunflower oil
6 bay leaves, torn into
  pieces
grated rind and juice
  of 2 lemons
125 ml/4 fl oz beer
1 tbsp clear honey
6 juniper berries, lightly
  crushed
salt and pepper
1 crisp dessert apple

Place the pork escalopes in a large, shallow, non-metallic dish. Heat the oil in a small, heavy-based saucepan. Add the bay leaves and stir-fry for 1 minute. Stir in the lemon rind and juice, beer, honey and juniper berries and season to taste with salt and pepper.

Pour the mixture over the pork, turning to coat. Cover with clingfilm, leave to cool, then leave to marinate in the refrigerator for up to 8 hours.

Preheat the barbecue. Drain the pork, reserving the marinade. Core the apple and cut into rings. Cook the pork over medium hot coals, brushing frequently with the reserved marinade, for 5 minutes on each side, or until thoroughly cooked. Cook the apples on the barbecue, brushing frequently with the marinade, for 3 minutes. Transfer the pork to a large serving plate with the apple rings and serve immediately.

pork with a medley of tropical fruit and spice

caribbean pork

serves 4

4 pork loin chops
4 tbsp dark muscovado
  sugar
4 tbsp orange or pineapple
  juice
2 tbsp Jamaican rum
1 tbsp desiccated coconut
½ tsp ground cinnamon
mixed salad leaves,
  to serve

coconut rice
225 g/8 oz basmati rice
450 ml/16 fl oz water
150 ml/5 fl oz coconut milk
4 tbsp raisins
4 tbsp roasted peanuts or
  cashew nuts
salt and pepper
2 tbsp desiccated coconut,
  toasted

Trim any excess fat from the pork and place the chops in a shallow, non-metallic dish. Mix the sugar, fruit juice, rum, coconut and cinnamon together in a bowl, stirring until the sugar dissolves. Pour the mixture over the pork, cover and leave to marinate in the refrigerator for at least 2 hours, or preferably overnight.

Preheat the barbecue. Remove the pork from the marinade, reserving the liquid for basting. Cook over hot coals for 15–20 minutes, basting with the marinade.

Meanwhile, make the coconut rice. Rinse the rice under cold running water, place it in a saucepan with the water and coconut milk and bring gently to the boil. Stir, cover and reduce the heat. Simmer gently for 12 minutes, or until the rice is tender and the liquid has been absorbed. Fluff up with a fork.

Stir the raisins and nuts into the rice, season to taste with salt and pepper and sprinkle with the coconut. Transfer the pork and rice to warmed serving plates and serve immediately with mixed salad leaves.

these golden spicy poussins are sure to impress

butterflied
poussins

serves 4

4 poussins, about
   450 g/1 lb each
1 tbsp paprika
1 tbsp mustard powder
1 tbsp ground cumin
pinch of cayenne pepper
1 tbsp tomato ketchup
1 tbsp lemon juice
salt
5 tbsp melted butter
fresh coriander sprigs,
   to garnish
corn on the cob, to serve

To butterfly the poussins, turn 1 bird breast-side down and, using strong kitchen scissors or poultry shears, cut through the skin and ribcage along both sides of the backbone, from tail to neck. Remove the backbone and turn the bird breast-side up. Press down firmly on the breastbone to flatten. Fold the wingtips underneath. Push a skewer through one wing, the top of the breast and out of the other wing. Push a second skewer through one thigh, the bottom of the breast and out through the other thigh. Repeat with the remaining poussins.

Mix the paprika, mustard powder, cumin, cayenne, tomato ketchup and lemon juice together in a small bowl and season to taste with salt. Gradually stir in the butter to make a smooth paste. Spread the paste evenly over the poussins, cover and leave to marinate in the refrigerator for up to 8 hours.

Preheat the barbecue. Cook the poussins over medium hot coals, turning frequently, for 25–30 minutes, brushing with a little oil if necessary. Transfer to a serving plate, garnish with fresh coriander sprigs and serve with corn on the cob.

tarragon and turkey form an ideal partnership

tarragon turkey

serves 4

4 turkey breasts, about
  175 g/6 oz each
salt and pepper
4 tsp wholegrain mustard
8 fresh tarragon sprigs,
  plus extra to garnish
4 smoked back bacon
  rashers
salad leaves, to serve

Preheat the barbecue. Season the turkey to taste with salt and pepper, and, using a round-bladed knife, spread the mustard evenly over the turkey.

Place 2 tarragon sprigs on top of each turkey breast and wrap a bacon rasher around it to hold the herbs in place. Secure with a cocktail stick.

Cook the turkey over medium hot coals for 5–8 minutes on each side. Transfer to serving plates and garnish with tarragon sprigs. Serve with salad leaves.

apricots are the perfect foil to the rich duck

fruity duck

serves 4

4 duck breasts
115 g/4 oz ready-to-eat
   dried apricots
2 shallots, thinly sliced
2 tbsp clear honey
1 tsp sesame oil
2 tsp Chinese five-spice
   powder

Preheat the barbecue. Using a sharp knife, cut a long slit in the fleshy side of each duck breast to make a pocket. Divide the apricots and shallots between the pockets and secure with skewers.

Mix the honey and sesame oil together in a small bowl and brush all over the duck. Sprinkle with the Chinese five-spice powder.

Cook the duck over medium hot coals for 6–8 minutes on each side. Remove the skewers, transfer to a large serving plate and serve immediately.

meaty and succulent monkfish is great for the barbecue

orange & lemon peppered **monkfish**

serves 8

2 oranges
2 lemons
2 monkfish tails, about
  500 g/1 lb 2 oz each,
  skinned and cut into
  4 fillets
8 fresh lemon thyme
  sprigs
2 tbsp olive oil
salt
2 tbsp green peppercorns,
  lightly crushed

Cut 8 orange slices and 8 lemon slices, reserving the remaining fruit. Rinse the monkfish fillets under cold running water and pat dry with kitchen paper. Place the monkfish fillets, cut side up, on a work surface and divide the citrus slices among them. Top with the lemon thyme. Tie each fillet at intervals with kitchen string to secure the citrus slices and thyme. Place the monkfish in a large, shallow, non-metallic dish.

Squeeze the juice from the remaining fruit and mix with the olive oil in a jug. Season to taste with salt, then spoon the mixture over the fish. Cover with clingfilm and leave to marinate in the refrigerator for up to 1 hour, spooning the marinade over the fish tails once or twice.

Preheat the barbecue. Drain the monkfish tails, reserving the marinade. Sprinkle the crushed green peppercorns over the fish, pressing them in with your fingers. Cook the monkfish over medium hot coals, turning and brushing frequently with the reserved marinade, for 20–25 minutes. Transfer to a chopping board, remove and discard the string and cut the monkfish tails into slices. Serve immediately.

an extra special fish dish with
Indonesian spices

baked red mullet

serves 4

4 banana leaves
2 limes
3 garlic cloves
4 red mullet, about
 350 g/12 oz each
2 spring onions,
 thinly sliced
2.5-cm/1-inch piece fresh
 root ginger
1 onion, finely chopped
4½ tsp groundnut or
 corn oil
3 tbsp kecap manis or
 light soy sauce
1 tsp ground coriander
1 tsp ground cumin
¼ tsp ground cloves
¼ tsp ground turmeric

Preheat the barbecue. If necessary, cut the banana leaves into
4 x 40-cm/16-inch squares, using a sharp knife or scissors.
Thinly slice 1½ limes and 1 garlic clove. Clean and scale the fish,
then rinse it inside and out under cold running water. Pat dry
with kitchen paper. Using a sharp knife, make a series of deep
diagonal slashes on the side of each fish, then insert the lime
and garlic slices into the slashes. Place the fish on the banana
leaf squares and sprinkle with the spring onions.

Finely chop the remaining garlic and squeeze the juice from the
remaining lime half. Finely chop the ginger, then place the garlic
in a bowl with the onion, ginger, oil, kecap manis, spices and lime
juice and mix to a paste.

Spoon the paste into the fish cavities and spread it over the
outside. Roll up the parcels and tie securely with string. Cook over
medium hot coals, turning occasionally, for 15–20 minutes. Serve.

these succulent prawns will be loved by all

prawns
with citrus salsa

serves 6

36 large, raw tiger prawns
2 tbsp finely chopped fresh
 coriander
pinch of cayenne pepper
3–4 tbsp corn oil
fresh coriander leaves,
 to garnish
lime wedges, to serve

salsa
1 orange
1 tart eating apple, peeled,
 quartered and cored
2 fresh red chillies,
 deseeded and chopped
1 garlic clove, chopped
8 fresh coriander sprigs
8 fresh mint sprigs
4 tbsp lime juice
salt and pepper

Preheat the barbecue. To make the salsa, peel the orange and cut into segments. Reserve any juice. Put the orange segments, apple quarters, chillies, garlic, coriander and mint into a food processor and process until smooth. With the motor running, add the lime juice through the feeder tube. Transfer the salsa to a serving bowl and season to taste with salt and pepper. Cover with clingfilm and leave to chill in the refrigerator until required.

Using a sharp knife, remove and discard the heads from the prawns, then peel off the shells. Cut along the back of the prawns and remove the dark intestinal vein. Rinse the prawns under cold running water and pat dry with kitchen paper. Mix the chopped coriander, cayenne and corn oil together in a dish. Add the prawns and toss well to coat.

Cook the prawns over medium hot coals for 3 minutes on each side, or until they have changed colour. Transfer to a large serving plate, garnish with fresh coriander leaves and serve immediately with lime wedges and the salsa.

this dish is simple to prepare and tastes delicious

stuffed sardines

serves 6

15 g/½ oz fresh parsley,
  finely chopped
4 garlic cloves, finely
  chopped
12 fresh sardines, cleaned
  and scaled
3 tbsp lemon juice
85 g/3 oz plain flour
1 tsp ground cumin
salt and pepper
olive oil, for brushing

Place the parsley and garlic in a bowl and mix together. Rinse the fish inside and out under cold running water and pat dry with kitchen paper. Spoon the herb mixture into the fish cavities and pat the remainder all over the outside of the fish. Sprinkle the sardines with lemon juice and transfer to a large, shallow, non-metallic dish. Cover with clingfilm and leave to marinate in the refrigerator for 1 hour.

Preheat the barbecue. Mix the flour and ground cumin together in a bowl, then season to taste with salt and pepper. Spread out the seasoned flour on a large plate and gently roll the sardines in the flour to coat.

Brush the sardines with olive oil and cook over medium hot coals for 3–4 minutes on each side. Serve immediately.

oysters and bacon make an appetising
delicacy

chargrilled
devils

serves 6

36 fresh oysters
18 streaky bacon rashers,
    rinded
1 tbsp mild paprika
1 tsp cayenne pepper

sauce
1 fresh red chilli, deseeded
    and finely chopped
1 garlic clove, finely
    chopped
1 shallot, finely chopped
2 tbsp finely chopped fresh
    parsley
2 tbsp lemon juice
salt and pepper

Preheat the barbecue. Open the oysters, catching the juice from the shells in a bowl. Cut the oysters from the bottom shells, reserve and tip any remaining juice into the bowl. To make the sauce, add the red chilli, garlic, shallot, parsley and lemon juice to the bowl, then season to taste with salt and pepper and mix well. Cover the bowl with clingfilm and leave to chill in the refrigerator until required.

Cut each bacon rasher in half across the centre. Season the oysters with paprika and cayenne, then roll each oyster up inside half a bacon rasher. Thread 6 wrapped oysters on to each of the 6 presoaked wooden skewers.

Cook over hot coals, turning frequently, for 5 minutes, or until the bacon is well browned and crispy. Transfer to a large serving plate and serve immediately with the sauce.

you can vary the filling of these tasty mushrooms

stuffed mushrooms

serves 12

12 open-cap mushrooms
4 tsp olive oil
4 spring onions, chopped
100 g/3½ oz fresh brown
   breadcrumbs
1 tsp chopped fresh
   oregano
100 g/3½ oz feta cheese or
   chorizo sausage
sunflower oil, for oiling

Preheat the barbecue. Remove the stalks from the mushrooms and chop the stalks finely. Heat half of the olive oil in a large frying pan. Add the mushroom stalks and spring onions and sauté briefly.

Mix the mushroom stalks and spring onions together in a large bowl. Add the breadcrumbs and oregano to the mushrooms and spring onions, mix well, then reserve until required.

If using feta, crumble the cheese into small pieces in a small bowl. If you are using chorizo sausage, remove the skin and chop the flesh finely.

Add the crumbled feta cheese or chopped chorizo to the breadcrumb mixture and mix well. Spoon the stuffing mixture into the mushroom caps.

Drizzle the remaining olive oil over the stuffed mushrooms, then cook on an oiled rack over medium hot coals for 8–10 minutes. Transfer the mushrooms to individual serving plates and serve while still hot.

courgettes and feta are a stunning combination

courgette &
cheese **parcels**

serves 2

1 small bunch of
  fresh mint
2 large courgettes
1 tbsp olive oil, plus extra
  for brushing
115 g/4 oz feta cheese,
  cut into strips
pepper

Preheat the barbecue. Using a sharp knife, finely chop enough mint to fill 1 tablespoon. Reserve until required. Cut out 2 rectangles of foil, each large enough to enclose a courgette, and brush lightly with olive oil. Cut a few slits along the length of each courgette and place them on the foil rectangles.

Insert strips of feta cheese along the slits in the courgettes, then drizzle the olive oil over the top, sprinkle with the reserved chopped mint and season to taste with pepper. Fold in the sides of the foil rectangles securely and seal the edges to enclose the cheese-stuffed courgettes completely.

Bake the courgette parcels in the barbecue embers for 30–40 minutes. Carefully unwrap the parcels and serve immediately.

stuffed tomato
parcels

serves 4

1 tbsp olive oil
2 tbsp sunflower seeds
1 onion, finely chopped
1 garlic clove, finely
  chopped
500 g/1 lb 2 oz fresh
  spinach, thick stalks
  removed and leaves
  shredded
pinch of freshly grated
  nutmeg
salt and pepper
4 beef tomatoes
140 g/5 oz mozzarella
  cheese, diced

Preheat the barbecue. Heat the oil in a heavy-based saucepan. Add the sunflower seeds and cook, stirring constantly, for 2 minutes, or until golden. Add the onion and cook over a low heat, stirring occasionally, for 5 minutes, or until softened but not browned. Add the garlic and spinach, cover and cook for 2–3 minutes, or until the spinach has wilted. Remove the saucepan from the heat and season to taste with nutmeg, salt and pepper. Leave to cool.

Using a sharp knife, cut off and reserve a thin slice from the top of each tomato and scoop out the flesh with a teaspoon, taking care not to pierce the shell. Chop the flesh and stir it into the spinach mixture with the mozzarella cheese.

Fill the tomato shells with the spinach and cheese mixture and replace the tops. Cut 4 squares of foil, each large enough to enclose a tomato. Place one tomato in the centre of each square and fold up the sides to enclose securely. Cook over hot coals, turning occasionally, for 10 minutes. Serve immediately in the foil parcels.

Burgers

this home-made burger is the ultimate barbecue treat

the classic
hamburger

· ·

serves 4–6

450 g/1 lb rump steak or
   topside, freshly minced
1 onion, grated
2–4 garlic cloves, crushed
2 tsp wholegrain mustard
pepper
2 tbsp olive oil
450 g/1 lb onions, finely
   sliced
2 tsp light muscovado
   sugar
hamburger buns, to serve

Place the minced steak, onion, garlic, mustard and pepper in a large bowl and mix together. Shape into 4–6 equal-sized burgers, then cover and leave to chill for 30 minutes.

Meanwhile, heat the oil in a heavy-based frying pan. Add the onions and sauté over a low heat for 10–15 minutes, or until the onions have caramelised. Add the sugar after 8 minutes and stir occasionally during cooking. Drain well on kitchen paper and keep warm.

Preheat the barbecue. Cook the burgers over hot coals for 3–5 minutes on each side or until cooked to personal preference. Serve in hamburger buns with the onions.

a tasty twist on the classic favourite dish

beef burgers
with chilli & basil

serves 4

650 g/1 lb 7 oz minced beef
1 red pepper, deseeded and
  finely chopped
1 garlic clove, finely
  chopped
2 small red chillies,
  deseeded and finely
  chopped
1 tbsp chopped fresh basil
½ tsp ground cumin
salt and pepper
sprigs of fresh basil,
  to garnish
hamburger buns, to serve

Put the minced beef, red pepper, garlic, chillies, chopped basil and cumin into a bowl and mix until well combined. Season with salt and pepper. Using your hands, form the mixture into burger shapes.

Preheat the barbecue. Cook the burgers over hot coals for 5–8 minutes on each side, or until cooked right through. Garnish with sprigs of basil and serve in hamburger buns.

pork burgers
with tangy orange marinade

serves 4–6

450 g/1 lb pork fillet,
  cut into small pieces
3 tbsp Seville orange
  marmalade
2 tbsp orange juice
1 tbsp balsamic vinegar
225 g/8 oz parsnips,
  cut into chunks
1 tbsp finely grated
  orange rind
2 garlic cloves, crushed
6 spring onions, finely
  chopped
1 courgette (175 g/6 oz),
  grated
salt and pepper
1 tbsp sunflower oil
lettuce leaves, to serve
hamburger buns, to serve

Place the pork in a shallow dish. Place the marmalade, orange juice and vinegar in a small saucepan and heat, stirring, until the marmalade has melted. Pour the marinade over the pork. Cover and leave for at least 30 minutes, or longer if time permits. Remove the pork, reserving the marinade. Mince the pork into a large bowl.

Meanwhile, cook the parsnips in a saucepan of boiling water for 15–20 minutes, or until cooked. Drain, then mash and add to the pork. Stir in the orange rind, garlic, spring onions, courgette and salt and pepper to taste. Mix together, then shape into 4–6 equal-sized burgers. Cover and leave to chill for at least 30 minutes.

Preheat the barbecue. Lightly brush each burger with a little oil and then add them to the barbecue grill, cooking over medium hot coals for 4–6 minutes on each side or until thoroughly cooked. Boil the reserved marinade for at least 5 minutes, then pour into a small jug or bowl. Serve with the lettuce leaves in hamburger buns.

cajun spices give this burger a
fabulous smoky tang

barbecued
cajun pork burgers

serves 4–6

225 g/8 oz sweet potatoes,
  cut into chunks
salt and pepper
450 g/1 lb fresh pork
  mince
1 Granny Smith or other
  eating apple, peeled,
  cored and grated
2 tsp Cajun seasoning
450 g/1 lb onions
1 tbsp chopped fresh
  coriander
2 tbsp sunflower oil
8–12 lean back bacon
  rashers

Cook the sweet potato in a saucepan of lightly salted boiling
water for 15–20 minutes, or until soft when pierced with a fork.
Drain well, then mash and reserve.

Place the pork mince in a bowl, add the mashed potato, grated
apple and Cajun seasoning. Grate 1 of the onions and add to the
mince mixture with salt and pepper to taste and the chopped
coriander. Mix together, then shape into 4–6 equal-sized burgers.
Cover and leave to chill for 1 hour.

Preheat the barbecue. Slice the remaining onions. Heat
1 tablespoon of the oil in a frying pan. Add the onions and
cook over a low heat for 10–12 minutes, stirring until soft.
Remove the frying pan from the heat and reserve. Wrap each
burger in 2 rashers of bacon.

Cook the burgers over hot coals, brushing with the remaining oil
for 4–5 minutes on each side, or until thoroughly cooked. Serve
with the fried onions.

minty lamb
burgers

serves 4–6

1 red pepper, deseeded and
  cut into quarters
1 yellow pepper, deseeded
  and cut into quarters
1 red onion, cut into thick
  wedges
1 baby aubergine (115 g/
  4 oz), cut into wedges
2 tbsp olive oil
450 g/1 lb fresh lamb
  mince
2 tbsp freshly grated
  Parmesan cheese
1 tbsp chopped fresh mint
salt and pepper

**minty mustard
mayonnaise**
4 tbsp mayonnaise
1 tsp Dijon mustard
1 tbsp chopped fresh mint

to serve
hamburger buns
shredded lettuce
grilled vegetables,
  such as peppers and
  cherry tomatoes

Preheat the grill to medium. Place the peppers, onion and
aubergine on a foil-lined grill rack, brush the aubergine
with 1 tablespoon of the oil and cook under the hot grill for
10–12 minutes, or until charred. Remove from the grill, leave
to cool, then peel the peppers. Place all the vegetables in a food
processor and, using the pulse button, chop.

Add the lamb mince, Parmesan cheese, chopped mint and salt
and pepper to the food processor and blend until the mixture
comes together. Scrape on to a board and shape into 4–6 equal-
sized burgers. Cover and leave to chill for at least 30 minutes.

To make the minty mustard mayonnaise, blend the mayonnaise
with the mustard and chopped fresh mint. Cover and chill
until required.

Preheat the barbecue. Lightly brush the burgers with the
remaining oil, and cook over hot coals for 3–4 minutes on each
side or until cooked to personal preference. Serve the burgers
in hamburger buns with the shredded lettuce and prepared
mayonnaise, and a selection of grilled vegetables on the side.

feta and pine nuts combine in this greek-style dish

lamb & feta
burgers

● ●

serves 4–6

450 g/1 lb fresh lamb
  mince
225 g/8 oz feta cheese,
  crumbled
2 garlic cloves, crushed
6 spring onions, finely
  chopped
85 g/3 oz ready-to-eat
  prunes, chopped
25 g/1 oz pine kernels,
  toasted
55 g/2 oz fresh wholemeal
  breadcrumbs
1 tbsp chopped fresh
  rosemary
salt and pepper
1 tbsp sunflower oil

Place the lamb mince in a large bowl with the feta, garlic, spring onions, prunes, pine kernels and breadcrumbs. Mix well, breaking up any lumps of mince.

Add the rosemary and salt and pepper to the lamb mixture in the bowl. Mix together, then shape into 4–6 equal-sized burgers. Cover and leave to chill for 30 minutes.

Preheat the barbecue. Brush the burgers lightly with oil and cook over hot coals for 4 minutes before turning over and brushing with the remaining oil. Continue to cook for 4 minutes, or until cooked to personal preference. Serve.

these breaded chicken burgers are deliciously tender

the ultimate
chicken burger

• •

serves 4

4 large chicken breast
  fillets, skinned
1 large egg white
1 tbsp cornflour
1 tbsp plain flour
1 egg, beaten
55 g/2 oz fresh white
  breadcrumbs
2 tbsp sunflower oil
2 beef tomatoes, sliced

to serve
hamburger buns
shredded lettuce
mayonnaise

Place the chicken breasts between 2 sheets of non-stick baking paper and flatten slightly using a meat mallet or a rolling pin. Beat the egg white and cornflour together, then brush over the chicken. Cover and leave to chill for 30 minutes, then coat in the flour.

Place the egg and breadcrumbs in 2 separate bowls and coat the burgers first in the egg, allowing any excess to drip back into the bowl, then in the breadcrumbs.

Preheat the barbecue. Lightly brush each burger with a little oil and then add them to the barbecue grill, cooking over medium hot coals for 6–8 minutes on each side, or until thoroughly cooked. If you are in doubt, it is worth cutting one of the burgers in half. If there is any sign of pinkness, cook for a little longer to get that nice barbecue taste. Add the tomato slices to the grill rack for the last 1–2 minutes of the cooking time to heat through. Serve the burgers in hamburger buns with the shredded lettuce, cooked tomato slices and mayonnaise.

burgers with a scrumptiously sticky maple glaze

maple-glazed
turkey burgers

serves 4

2 corn on the cob with
  leaves intact
450 g/1 lb fresh turkey
  mince
1 red pepper, deseeded,
  peeled and finely
  chopped
6 spring onions, finely
  chopped
55 g/2 oz fresh white
  breadcrumbs
2 tbsp chopped fresh basil
salt and pepper
1 tbsp sunflower oil
2 tbsp maple syrup

to serve
hamburger buns
salad leaves
tomato slices

Heat a griddle pan until hot, then add the corn on the cob and cook over a medium-high heat for 8–10 minutes, turning every 2–3 minutes, or until the leaves are charred. Remove from the griddle pan, leave to cool, then strip off the leaves and silky threads. Using a sharp knife, cut away the kernels and place in a bowl.

Add the turkey mince, red pepper, spring onions, breadcrumbs, basil, salt and pepper to the sweetcorn kernels in the bowl. Mix together, then shape into 4 equal-sized burgers. Cover and leave to chill for 1 hour.

Preheat the barbecue. Brush the burgers lightly with oil, glaze with half of the maple syrup and cook over hot coals for 4 minutes. Turn over the burgers and brush with the remaining oil and maple syrup and continue to cook for 4 minutes, or until cooked to personal preference. Serve the burgers in hamburger buns with the salad leaves and tomato slices.

an inspiring variation on the traditional fish cake

fish burgers

serves 4

140 g/5 oz potatoes,
  cut into chunks
salt and pepper
225 g/8 oz cod fillet,
  skinned
225 g/8 oz smoked
  haddock, skinned
1 tbsp grated lemon rind
1 tbsp chopped fresh
  parsley
1–2 tbsp plain flour
1 egg, beaten
85 g/3 oz fresh white
  breadcrumbs
2 tbsp sunflower oil
hamburger buns, to serve

Cook the potatoes in a saucepan of lightly salted boiling water for 15–20 minutes, or until tender. Drain well and mash. Chop the fish into small pieces, then place in a food processor with the mashed potatoes, lemon rind, parsley and salt and pepper to taste. Using the pulse button, blend together. Shape into 4 equal-sized burgers and coat in flour. Cover and leave to chill for 30 minutes.

Place the egg and breadcrumbs in 2 separate bowls and coat the burgers first in the egg, allowing any excess to drip back into the bowl, then in the breadcrumbs. Leave to chill for a further 30 minutes.

Preheat the barbecue. Brush the burgers lightly with oil and cook over hot coals for 4–5 minutes on each side, or until golden and cooked through. Serve in toasted hamburger buns.

tuna burgers
with mango salsa

serves 4–6

225 g/8 oz sweet potatoes, chopped
salt
450 g/1 lb fresh tuna steaks
6 spring onions, finely chopped
175 g/6 oz courgette, grated
1 fresh red jalapeño chilli, deseeded and finely chopped
2 tbsp prepared mango chutney
1 tbsp sunflower oil
lettuce leaves, to serve

mango salsa

1 large ripe mango, peeled and stoned
2 ripe tomatoes, finely chopped
1 fresh red jalapeño chilli, deseeded and finely chopped
4-cm/1½-inch piece cucumber, finely diced
1 tbsp chopped fresh coriander
1–2 tsp clear honey

Cook the sweet potatoes in a saucepan of lightly salted boiling water for 15–20 minutes, or until tender. Drain well, then mash and place in a food processor. Cut the tuna into chunks and add to the potatoes.

Add the spring onions, courgette, chilli and mango chutney to the food processor and, using the pulse button, blend together. Shape into 4–6 equal-sized burgers, then cover and leave to chill for 1 hour.

Meanwhile make the salsa. Slice the mango flesh, reserving 8–12 good slices for serving. Finely chop the remainder, then mix with the tomatoes, chilli, cucumber, coriander and honey. Mix well, then spoon into a small bowl. Cover and leave for 30 minutes to allow the flavours to develop.

Preheat the barbecue. Brush the burgers lightly with oil and cook over hot coals for 4–6 minutes on each side, or until piping hot. Serve with the mango salsa, garnished with lettuce leaves and the reserved slices of mango.

a winning combination of rice, beans and nuts

the ultimate
vegetarian burger

serves 4–6

85 g/3 oz brown rice
salt and pepper
400 g/14 oz canned
  flageolet beans, drained
115 g/4 oz unsalted
  cashew nuts
3 garlic cloves
1 red onion, cut into
  wedges
115 g/4 oz sweetcorn
  kernels
2 tbsp tomato purée
1 tbsp chopped fresh
  oregano
2 tbsp wholemeal flour
2 tbsp sunflower oil

to serve
hamburger buns
lettuce leaves
tomato slices
cheese slices

Preheat the barbecue. Cook the rice in a saucepan of lightly salted boiling water for 20 minutes, or until tender. Drain and place in a food processor.

Add the beans, cashew nuts, garlic, onion, sweetcorn, tomato purée, oregano and salt and pepper to the rice in the food processor and, using the pulse button, blend together. Shape into 4–6 equal-sized burgers, then coat in the flour. Cover and leave to chill for 1 hour.

Lightly brush the burgers with oil. When the barbecue is hot, cook the burgers over medium hot coals for 5–6 minutes on each side or until cooked and piping hot. Serve the burgers in hamburger buns with the salad leaves, and tomato and cheese slices.

three-bean burgers
with green mayo

serves 4–6

300 g/10½ oz canned
cannellini beans, drained
300 g/10½ oz canned
black-eyed beans,
drained
300 g/10½ oz canned red
kidney beans, drained
and rinsed
1 fresh red chilli, deseeded
4 shallots, cut into
quarters
2 celery sticks, roughly
chopped
55 g/2 oz fresh wholemeal
breadcrumbs
1 tbsp chopped fresh
coriander
salt and pepper
2 tbsp wholemeal flour
2 tbsp sunflower oil
hamburger buns, to serve

green mayo
6 tbsp prepared
mayonnaise
2 tbsp chopped fresh
parsley or mint
1 tbsp chopped cucumber
3 spring onions, finely
chopped

Place the beans, chilli, shallots, celery, breadcrumbs, coriander and salt and pepper in a food processor and, using the pulse button, blend together. Shape into 4–6 equal-sized burgers, then cover and leave to chill for 1 hour. Coat the burgers lightly in the flour.

To make the green mayo, place the mayonnaise, parsley, cucumber and spring onions in a bowl and mix together. Cover and chill until required.

Preheat the barbecue. Brush the burgers lightly with oil and cook over hot coals for 5–6 minutes on each side, or until piping hot. Serve in hamburger buns with the green mayo.

these burgers may be lacking in meat but not in flavour

mushroom
burgers

· ·

serves 4

115 g/4 oz mushrooms
1 carrot
1 onion
1 courgette
2 tsp sunflower oil, plus
   extra for brushing
25 g/1 oz peanuts
115 g/4 oz fresh white
   breadcrumbs
1 tbsp chopped fresh
   parsley
1 tsp yeast extract
salt and pepper
1 tbsp plain flour,
   for dusting

Using a sharp knife, finely chop the mushrooms, then chop the carrot, onion and courgette and reserve. Heat the oil in a heavy-based frying pan, add the mushrooms and cook, stirring, for 8 minutes, or until all the moisture has evaporated. Using a slotted spoon, transfer the cooked mushrooms to a large bowl.

Put the carrot, onion, courgette and peanuts into a food processor and process until finely chopped. Transfer to the bowl containing the mushrooms and stir in the breadcrumbs, chopped parsley and yeast extract. Season to taste with salt and pepper. Lightly flour your hands and form the mixture into 4 patties. Place on a large plate, cover with clingfilm and leave to chill in the refrigerator for at least 1 hour and up to 1 day.

Preheat the barbecue. Brush the mushroom burgers with the sunflower oil and cook over hot coals for 8–10 minutes. Serve.

Skewers

this is a barbecue version of the classic dish

surf 'n' turf

skewers

●●●

serves 2

225 g/8 oz fillet steak,
  about 2.5-cm/1-inch
  thick
8 raw unpeeled tiger
  prawns
olive oil, for oiling
salt and pepper
4 tbsp butter
2 garlic cloves, crushed
3 tbsp chopped fresh
  parsley, plus extra
  parsley sprigs,
  to garnish
finely grated rind and
  juice of 1 lime
lime wedges, to garnish
crusty bread, to serve

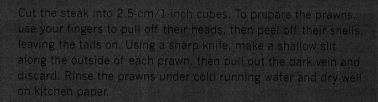

Cut the steak into 2.5-cm/1-inch cubes. To prepare the prawns, use your fingers to pull off their heads, then peel off their shells, leaving the tails on. Using a sharp knife, make a shallow slit along the outside of each prawn, then pull out the dark vein and discard. Rinse the prawns under cold running water and dry well on kitchen paper.

Thread an equal number of the steak cubes and prawns on to 2 oiled metal kebab skewers or presoaked wooden skewers. Season the kebabs to taste with pepper.

Preheat the barbecue. Meanwhile, put the butter and garlic into a small saucepan and heat gently until melted. Remove from the heat and add the parsley, lime rind and juice and salt and pepper to taste. Leave in a warm place so that the butter remains melted.

Brush the kebabs with a little of the melted butter. Put the kebabs on to an oiled grill rack and cook over hot coals for 4–8 minutes until the steak is cooked according to your taste and the prawns turn pink, turning the kebabs frequently during cooking, and brushing with the remaining melted butter.

Serve the kebabs hot on the skewers, with the remaining butter spooned over. Garnish with lime wedges and parsley sprigs and serve with crusty bread to mop up the buttery juices.

beef in a classic japanese-style marinade

beef teriyaki

● ●

serves 4

450 g/1 lb extra thin beef
   steaks
1 yellow pepper, deseeded
   and cut into chunks
8 spring onions, trimmed
   and cut into short
   lengths
salad leaves, to serve

sauce

1 tsp cornflour
2 tbsp dry sherry
2 tbsp white wine vinegar
3 tbsp soy sauce
1 tbsp dark muscovado
   sugar
1 garlic clove, crushed
½ tsp ground cinnamon
½ tsp ground ginger

Place the beef steaks in a shallow, non-metallic dish. To make the sauce, mix the cornflour and sherry together in a small bowl, then stir in the remaining sauce ingredients. Pour the sauce over the meat, cover with clingfilm and leave to marinate in the refrigerator for at least 2 hours.

Preheat the barbecue. Remove the meat from the sauce and reserve. Pour the sauce into a small saucepan and boil for at least 5 minutes, stirring occasionally.

Cut the meat into thin strips and thread these, concertina-style, on to several presoaked wooden skewers, alternating each strip of meat with the pieces of pepper and spring onion. Cook the kebabs over hot coals for 5–8 minutes, turning and basting the beef and vegetables occasionally with the reserved sauce.

Arrange the skewers on serving plates and pour over the remaining sauce. Serve with salad leaves.

spicy meat patties moulded around kebab skewers

indian kofta

●●●

serves 4

1 small onion
450 g/1 lb fresh lean lamb
   mince
2 tbsp curry paste
2 tbsp natural yogurt
sunflower oil, for basting

tomato sambal
3 tomatoes, deseeded
   and diced
pinch of ground coriander
pinch of ground cumin
2 tsp chopped fresh
   coriander
salt and pepper

to serve
poppadums
chutney

Place the onion in a food processor and chop finely. Add the lamb and process briefly to chop the mince further. Chopping the mince again will help the meat mixture to hold together during cooking. Alternatively, grate the onion finely before mixing it with the lamb.

Add the curry paste and yogurt and mix well. Divide the mixture into 8 equal-sized portions. Press and shape the mixture into 8 sausage shapes and push each one on to a metal or presoaked wooden skewer, pressing the mixture together firmly so that it holds its shape. Leave to chill in the refrigerator for at least 30 minutes, or until required.

To make the tomato sambal, mix the tomatoes, spices, chopped coriander and salt and pepper to taste together in a bowl. Leave to stand for at least 30 minutes for the flavours to combine.

Preheat the barbecue. Cook the kebabs on an oiled rack over hot coals for 10–15 minutes, turning frequently. Baste with a little sunflower oil if required. Serve accompanied with poppadums, chutney and the tomato sambal.

these fragrant kebabs are a georgian speciality

shashlik

• •

serves 4

675 g/1 lb 8 oz boneless
   leg of lamb, cut into
   2.5-cm/1-inch cubes
12 large mushrooms
4 streaky bacon rashers,
   rinded
8 cherry tomatoes
1 large green pepper,
   deseeded and cut into
   squares
crusty bread, to serve

marinade
4 tbsp sunflower oil
4 tbsp lemon juice
1 onion, finely chopped
½ tsp dried rosemary
½ tsp dried thyme
salt and pepper

Place the lamb and mushrooms in a large, shallow, non-metallic dish. Mix all the ingredients for the marinade together in a jug, seasoning to taste with salt and pepper. Pour the mixture over the lamb and mushrooms, turning to coat. Cover with clingfilm and leave to marinate in the refrigerator for up to 8 hours.

Preheat the barbecue. Cut the bacon rashers in half across the centre and stretch with a heavy, flat-bladed knife, then roll up. Drain the lamb and mushrooms, reserving the marinade. Thread the bacon rolls, lamb, mushrooms, tomatoes and green pepper squares alternately on to metal skewers. Sieve the marinade.

Cook the kebabs over medium hot coals, turning and brushing frequently with the reserved marinade, for 10–15 minutes. Transfer to a large serving plate and serve immediately with crusty bread.

a classic combination of pork and apple

normandy
brochettes

• •

serves 4

450 g/1 lb pork fillet
300 ml/10 fl oz dry cider
1 tbsp finely chopped fresh
  sage
6 black peppercorns,
  crushed
2 crisp eating apples
1 tbsp sunflower oil
crusty bread, to serve

Using a sharp knife, cut the pork into 2.5-cm/1-inch cubes, then place in a large, shallow, non-metallic dish. Mix the cider, sage and peppercorns together in a jug, pour the mixture over the pork and turn until thoroughly coated. Cover with clingfilm and leave to marinate in the refrigerator for 1–2 hours.

Preheat the barbecue. Drain the pork, reserving the marinade. Core the apples, but do not peel, then cut into wedges. Dip the apple wedges into the reserved marinade and thread on to several metal skewers, alternating with the cubes of pork. Stir the sunflower oil into the remaining marinade.

Cook the brochettes over medium hot coals, turning and brushing frequently with the reserved marinade, for 12–15 minutes. Transfer to a large serving plate and if you prefer, remove the meat and apples from the skewers before serving. Serve immediately with crusty bread.

these slightly sweet skewers are popular with children

pork & sage
kebabs

• •

serves 4

450 g/1 lb pork mince
25 g/1 oz fresh
   breadcrumbs
1 small onion, chopped
   very finely
1 tbsp fresh sage, chopped
2 tbsp apple sauce
¼ tsp ground nutmeg
salt and pepper

baste
3 tbsp olive oil
1 tbsp lemon juice

to serve
4 small pitta breads
mixed salad leaves
6 tbsp thick, natural
   yogurt

Place the mince in a mixing bowl together with the breadcrumbs, onion, sage, apple sauce, nutmeg and salt and pepper to taste. Mix until the ingredients are well combined.

Using your hands, shape the mixture into small balls, about the size of large marbles, and leave to chill in the refrigerator for at least 30 minutes.

Meanwhile, soak several small wooden skewers in cold water for at least 30 minutes. Thread the meatballs on to the skewers.

To make the baste, mix together the oil and lemon juice in a small bowl, whisking with a fork until it is well blended.

Barbecue the kebabs over hot coals for 8–10 minutes, turning and basting frequently with the lemon and oil mixture, until the meat is golden and cooked through.

Line the pitta breads with the salad leaves and spoon over some of the yogurt. Serve with the kebabs.

chicken in a zingy marinade of citrus juice and rind

zesty kebabs

• •

serves 4

4 skinless, boneless
  chicken breasts, about
  175 g/6 oz each
finely grated rind and
  juice of ½ lemon
finely grated rind and
  juice of ½ orange
2 tbsp clear honey
2 tbsp olive oil
2 tbsp chopped fresh mint,
  plus extra to garnish
¼ tsp ground coriander
salt and pepper
citrus zest, to garnish

Using a sharp knife, cut the chicken into 2.5-cm/1-inch cubes, then place them in a large glass bowl. Place the lemon and orange rind, the lemon and orange juice, the honey, oil, mint and ground coriander in a jug and mix together. Season to taste with salt and pepper. Pour the marinade over the chicken cubes and toss until they are thoroughly coated. Cover with clingfilm and leave to marinate in the refrigerator for up to 8 hours.

Preheat the barbecue. Drain the chicken cubes, reserving the marinade. Thread the chicken on to several long metal skewers.

Cook the skewers over medium hot coals, turning and brushing frequently with the reserved marinade, for 6–10 minutes, or until thoroughly cooked. Transfer to a large serving plate, garnish with fresh chopped mint and citrus zest and serve immediately.

these chicken skewers are wonderfully aromatic

chicken satay

● ●

serves 4

8 tbsp crunchy peanut butter
1 onion, roughly chopped
1 garlic clove, roughly chopped
2 tbsp creamed coconut
4 tbsp groundnut oil
1 tsp light soy sauce
2 tbsp lime juice
2 fresh red chillies, deseeded and chopped
3 kaffir lime leaves, torn
4 skinless, boneless chicken breasts, about 175 g/6 oz each, cut into 2.5-cm/1-inch cubes

Put the peanut butter, onion, garlic, coconut, groundnut oil, soy sauce, lime juice, chillies and lime leaves into a food processor and process to a smooth paste. Transfer the paste to a large glass bowl.

Add the chicken cubes to the dish and stir to coat thoroughly. Cover with clingfilm and leave to marinate in the refrigerator for up to 8 hours.

Preheat the barbecue. Thread the chicken cubes on to several presoaked wooden skewers, reserving the marinade. Cook the skewers over medium hot coals, turning and brushing frequently with the marinade, for 10 minutes, or until thoroughly cooked. Transfer to a large serving plate and serve immediately.

these are full of fabulous
mediterranean flavours

turkey
with coriander pesto

serves 4

450 g/1 lb skinless,
  boneless turkey, cut into
  5-cm/2-inch cubes
2 courgettes, thickly sliced
1 red and 1 yellow pepper,
  deseeded and cut into
  5-cm/2-inch squares
8 cherry tomatoes
8 baby onions, peeled but
  left whole

marinade
6 tbsp olive oil
3 tbsp dry white wine
1 tsp green peppercorns,
  crushed
2 tbsp chopped fresh
  coriander
salt

coriander pesto
55 g/2 oz fresh coriander
  leaves
15 g/½ oz fresh parsley
  leaves
1 garlic clove
55 g/2 oz pine kernels
25 g/1 oz freshly grated
  Parmesan cheese
6 tbsp extra-virgin olive oil
juice of 1 lemon

Place the turkey in a large glass bowl. To make the marinade,
mix the olive oil, wine, peppercorns and coriander together in
a jug and season to taste with salt. Pour the mixture over the
turkey and turn until the turkey is thoroughly coated. Cover with
clingfilm and leave to marinate in the refrigerator for 2 hours.

Preheat the barbecue. To make the pesto, put the coriander
and parsley into a food processor and process until finely
chopped. Add the garlic and pine kernels and pulse until
chopped. Add the Parmesan cheese, oil and lemon juice and
process briefly to mix. Transfer to a bowl, cover and leave to
chill in the refrigerator until required.

Drain the turkey, reserving the marinade. Thread the turkey,
courgette slices, pepper pieces, cherry tomatoes and onions
alternately on to metal skewers. Cook over medium hot coals,
turning and brushing frequently with the marinade, for
10 minutes. Serve immediately with the coriander pesto.

caribbean fish
kebabs

· ·

serves 6

1 kg/2 lb 4 oz swordfish
  steaks
3 tbsp olive oil
3 tbsp lime juice
1 garlic clove, finely
  chopped
1 tsp paprika
salt and pepper
3 onions, cut into wedges
6 tomatoes, cut into
  wedges

Using a sharp knife, cut the fish into 2.5-cm/1-inch cubes and place in a shallow, non-metallic dish. Place the oil, lime juice, garlic and paprika in a jug and mix well. Season to taste with salt and pepper. Pour the marinade over the fish, turning to coat. Cover with clingfilm and leave to marinate in the refrigerator for 1 hour.

Preheat the barbecue. Thread the fish cubes, onion wedges and tomato wedges alternately on to 6 long, presoaked wooden skewers. Reserve the marinade.

Cook the kebabs over medium hot coals for 8–10 minutes, turning and brushing frequently with the reserved marinade. When they are cooked through, transfer the kebabs to a large serving plate and serve immediately.

juicy prawns combined with delicate thai flavours

coconut prawns

· ·

serves 4

8 spring onions
400 ml/14 fl oz coconut
  milk
finely grated rind and
  juice of 1 lime
4 tbsp chopped fresh
  coriander, plus extra
  to garnish
2 tbsp corn or sunflower
  oil
pepper
650 g/1 lb 7 oz raw tiger
  prawns
lemon wedges, to garnish

Finely chop the spring onions and place in a large, shallow, non-metallic dish with the coconut milk, lime rind and juice, coriander and oil. Mix well and season to taste with pepper. Add the prawns, turning to coat. Cover with clingfilm and leave to marinate in the refrigerator for 1 hour.

Preheat the barbecue. Drain the prawns, reserving the marinade. Thread the prawns on to 8 long metal skewers.

Cook the skewers over medium hot coals, brushing with the reserved marinade and turning frequently, for 8 minutes, or until they have changed colour. Serve the prawns immediately, garnished with the lemon wedges and chopped coriander.

greek vegetable
kebabs

• •

serves 4

2 onions
8 new potatoes, washed
 but not peeled
salt
1 aubergine, cut into
 8 pieces
8 thick slices cucumber
1 red pepper, deseeded and
 cut into 8 pieces
1 yellow pepper, deseeded
 and cut into 8 pieces
225 g/8 oz halloumi
 cheese, cut into 8 cubes
2 nectarines, stoned and
 cut into wedges
8 button mushrooms
2 tbsp olive oil
2 tsp chopped fresh thyme
2 tsp chopped fresh
 rosemary
1 quantity cucumber
 and yogurt dip
 (see page 180), to serve

Preheat the barbecue. Cut the onions into wedges, then place the onions and potatoes in a saucepan of lightly salted boiling water and cook for 20 minutes, or until just tender. Drain and leave to cool. Meanwhile, blanch the aubergine in boiling water for 2 minutes, then add the cucumber and simmer for 1 minute. Add the peppers and simmer for a further 2 minutes, then drain and leave the vegetables to cool.

Place the cooled vegetables, cheese, nectarines and mushrooms in a bowl. Add the olive oil and herbs and toss to coat. Thread the vegetables, cheese, nectarines and mushrooms on to several metal skewers.

Cook the kebabs over hot coals, turning frequently, for 15 minutes. Transfer to a large serving plate and serve immediately with the cucumber and yogurt dip.

these kebabs are perfect for any vegetarian guests

marinated tofu
skewers

● ●

serves 4

350 g/12 oz firm tofu
1 red pepper
1 yellow pepper
2 courgettes
8 button mushrooms

marinade
grated rind and
  juice of ½ lemon
1 garlic clove, crushed
½ tsp chopped fresh
  rosemary
½ tsp chopped fresh
  thyme
1 tbsp walnut oil

to garnish
shredded carrot
lemon wedges

To make the marinade, mix the lemon rind and juice, garlic, rosemary, thyme and walnut oil together in a shallow dish. Drain the tofu, pat it dry on kitchen paper and cut it into squares. Add to the marinade and toss to coat. Leave to marinate for 20–30 minutes.

Preheat the barbecue. Deseed the peppers and cut into 2.5-cm/ 1-inch pieces. Blanch in boiling water for 4 minutes, refresh in cold water and drain. Using a canelle knife or potato peeler, remove strips of peel from the courgettes. Cut the courgettes into 2.5-cm/1-inch chunks.

Remove the tofu from the marinade, reserving the liquid for basting. Thread the tofu on to 8 presoaked wooden skewers, alternating with the peppers, courgette and button mushrooms.

Cook the skewers over medium hot coals for 6 minutes, turning and basting with the marinade. Transfer the skewers to warmed serving plates, garnish with shredded carrot and lemon wedges and serve.

Sides
& Sauces

crispy potato skins

serves 4–6

8 small baking potatoes,
   scrubbed
50 g/1¾ oz butter, melted
salt and pepper

optional topping
6 spring onions, sliced
50 g/1¾ oz grated
   Gruyère cheese
50 g/1¾ oz salami,
   cut into thin strips

Preheat the oven to 200°C/400°F/Gas Mark 6. Prick the potatoes with a fork and bake for 1 hour, or until tender. Alternatively, cook in a microwave on High for 12–15 minutes. Cut the potatoes in half and scoop out the flesh, leaving about 5 mm/¼ inch potato flesh lining the skin.

Preheat the barbecue. Brush the insides of the potato with melted butter.

Place the skins, cut-side down, over medium hot coals and cook for 10–15 minutes. Turn the potato skins over and barbecue for a further 5 minutes, or until they are crispy. Take care that they do not burn. Season the potato skins with salt and pepper to taste and serve while they are still warm.

If wished, the skins can be filled with a variety of toppings. Barbecue the potato skins as above for 10 minutes, then turn cut-side up and sprinkle with slices of spring onion, grated cheese and chopped salami. Barbecue for a further 5 minutes, or until the cheese begins to melt. Serve hot.

barbecuing transforms potatoes into tempting treats

potato fans

serves 6

6 large potatoes, scrubbed
  but not peeled
1 garlic clove, finely
  chopped
2 tbsp olive oil
salt and pepper

Preheat the barbecue. Using a sharp knife, make a series of cuts across the potatoes almost all the way through. Cut out 6 squares of foil, each large enough to enclose a potato, and place a potato on top of each one.

Mix together the garlic and olive oil and brush generously over the potatoes. Season with salt and pepper to taste. Fold up the sides of the foil to enclose the potatoes completely.

Cook over hot coals, turning occasionally, for 1 hour. To serve, open the foil parcels and gently pinch the potatoes to open up the fans.

chilli and lime give this side dish a spicy kick

pumpkin parcels
with chilli & lime

serves 4

700 g/1 lb 9 oz pumpkin
  or squash
2 tbsp sunflower oil
25 g/1 oz butter
½ tsp chilli sauce
grated rind of 1 lime
2 tsp lime juice

Preheat the barbecue. Halve the pumpkin or squash and scoop out the seeds. Rinse the seeds and reserve. Cut the pumpkin into thin wedges and peel.

Heat the sunflower oil and butter together in a large saucepan, stirring, until melted. Stir in the chilli sauce, lime rind and juice. Add the pumpkin and seeds to the saucepan and toss to coat on all sides in the flavoured butter.

Divide the mixture among 4 double-thickness sheets of foil. Fold over the foil to enclose the pumpkin mixture completely.

Cook the foil parcels over hot coals for 15–25 minutes, or until the pumpkin is tender. Transfer the foil parcels to warmed serving plates. Open the parcels at the table and serve immediately.

garlic bread

serves 6

150 g/5½ oz butter,
  softened
3 cloves garlic, crushed
2 tbsp chopped fresh
  parsley
pepper
1 large or 2 small sticks of
  French bread

Mix together the butter, garlic and parsley in a bowl until well combined. Season with pepper to taste and mix well.

Cut a few lengthwise slits in the French bread. Spread the flavoured butter inside the slits and place the bread on a large sheet of thick kitchen foil.

Preheat the barbecue. Wrap the bread well in the foil and barbecue over hot coals for 10–15 minutes until the butter melts and the bread is piping hot.

Serve as an accompaniment to a wide range of dishes.

juicy corn cobs with a delicious herb butter

corn on the cob

· ·

serves 4

4 corn cobs, with husks
100 g/3½ oz butter
1 tbsp chopped fresh
   parsley
1 tsp chopped fresh chives
1 tsp chopped fresh thyme
grated rind of 1 lemon
salt and pepper

Preheat the barbecue. To prepare the corn cobs, peel back the husks and remove the silken hairs. Fold back the husks and secure them in place with string if necessary.

Blanch the corn cobs in a large saucepan of boiling water for 5 minutes. Remove the corn cobs with a slotted spoon and drain thoroughly. Cook the corn cobs over medium hot coals for 20–30 minutes, turning frequently.

Meanwhile, soften the butter and beat in the parsley, chives, thyme, lemon rind and salt and pepper to taste. Transfer the corn cobs to serving plates, remove the string and pull back the husks. Serve each with a generous portion of herb butter.

barbecued vegetables with a fabulous pesto dip

chargrilled vegetables
with creamy pesto

serves 4

1 red onion
1 fennel bulb
4 baby aubergines
4 baby courgettes
1 orange pepper
1 red pepper
2 beef tomatoes
2 tbsp olive oil
salt and pepper
1 fresh basil sprig,
   to garnish

creamy pesto
55 g/2 oz fresh basil leaves
15 g/½ oz pine kernels
1 garlic clove
pinch of coarse sea salt
25 g/1 oz freshly grated
   Parmesan cheese
50 ml/2 fl oz extra-virgin
   olive oil
150 ml/5 fl oz natural
   Greek yogurt

Preheat the barbecue. To make the creamy pesto, place the basil, pine kernels, garlic and sea salt in a mortar and pound to a paste with a pestle. Gradually work in the Parmesan cheese, then gradually stir in the oil.

Place the yogurt in a small serving bowl and stir in 3–4 tablespoons of the pesto mixture. Cover with clingfilm and leave to chill in the refrigerator until required. Store any leftover pesto mixture in a screw-top jar in the refrigerator.

Prepare the vegetables. Cut the onion and fennel bulb into wedges, trim and slice the aubergines and courgettes, deseed and thickly slice the peppers and cut the tomatoes in half. Brush the vegetables with oil and season to taste with salt and pepper.

Cook the aubergines and peppers over hot coals for 3 minutes, then add the courgettes, onion, fennel and tomatoes and cook, turning occasionally and brushing with more oil if necessary, for a further 5 minutes. Transfer to a large serving plate and serve immediately with the pesto, garnished with a basil sprig.

summer vegetable **parcels**

serves 4

1 kg/2 lb 4 oz mixed baby
  vegetables, such as
  carrots, asparagus, corn
  cobs, plum tomatoes,
  leeks, courgettes,
  chillies and onions
1 lemon
115 g/4 oz unsalted butter
3 tbsp chopped mixed
  fresh herbs, such as
  parsley, thyme, chives
  and chervil
2 garlic cloves
salt and pepper

Preheat the barbecue. Cut out 4 x 30-cm/12-inch squares of foil and divide the vegetables equally among them.

Using a grater, finely grate the lemon rind, then squeeze the juice from the lemon and reserve until required. Put the lemon rind, butter, herbs and garlic into a food processor and process until blended, then season to taste with salt and pepper. Alternatively, beat together in a bowl until blended.

Divide the butter equally among the vegetables parcels, dotting it on top. Fold up the sides of the foil to enclose the vegetables, sealing securely. Cook over medium hot coals, turning occasionally, for 25–30 minutes. Open the parcels, sprinkle with the reserved lemon juice and serve immediately.

tropical rice salad

serves 4

115 g/4 oz long-grain rice
salt and pepper
4 spring onions
225 g/8 oz canned
  pineapple pieces in
  natural juice
200 g/7 oz canned
  sweetcorn, drained
2 red peppers, deseeded
  and diced
3 tbsp sultanas

dressing
1 tbsp groundnut oil
1 tbsp hazelnut oil
1 tbsp light soy sauce
1 garlic clove, finely
  chopped
1 tsp chopped fresh root
  ginger

Cook the rice in a large saucepan of lightly salted boiling water for 15 minutes, or until tender. Drain thoroughly and rinse under cold running water. Place the rice in a large serving bowl.

Using a sharp knife, finely chop the spring onions. Drain the pineapple pieces, reserving the juice in a jug. Add the pineapple pieces, sweetcorn, red peppers, chopped spring onions and sultanas to the rice and mix lightly.

Add all the dressing ingredients to the reserved pineapple juice, whisking well, and season to taste with salt and pepper. Pour the dressing over the salad and toss until the salad is thoroughly coated. Serve immediately.

tabbouleh

serves 4

175 g/6 oz bulgar wheat
3 tbsp extra-virgin olive oil
4 tbsp lemon juice
salt and pepper
4 spring onions
1 green pepper, deseeded
    and sliced
4 tomatoes, chopped
2 tbsp chopped fresh
    parsley
2 tbsp chopped fresh mint
8 black olives, stoned
fresh mint sprigs,
    to garnish

Place the bulgar wheat in a large bowl and add enough cold water to cover. Leave to stand for 30 minutes, or until the wheat has doubled in size. Drain well and press out as much liquid as possible. Spread out the wheat on kitchen paper to dry.

Place the wheat in a serving bowl. Mix the olive oil and lemon juice together in a jug and season to taste with salt and pepper. Pour the lemon mixture over the wheat and leave to marinate for 1 hour.

Using a sharp knife, finely chop the spring onions, then add to the salad with the green pepper, tomatoes, parsley and mint and toss lightly to mix. Top the salad with the olives and garnish with fresh mint sprigs, then serve.

pasta salad
with basil vinaigrette

serves 4

225 g/8 oz dried fusilli
salt and pepper
4 tomatoes
50 g/1¾ oz black olives
25 g/1 oz sun-dried
   tomatoes in oil
2 tbsp pine kernels
2 tbsp freshly grated
   Parmesan cheese
fresh basil leaves,
   to garnish

vinaigrette

15 g/½ oz basil leaves
1 garlic clove, crushed
2 tbsp freshly grated
   Parmesan cheese
4 tbsp extra-virgin olive oil
2 tbsp lemon juice

Cook the pasta in a large saucepan of lightly salted boiling water for 10–12 minutes, or until just tender but still firm to the bite. Drain the pasta, rinse under cold running water, then drain again thoroughly. Place the pasta in a large bowl.

Preheat the grill to medium. To make the vinaigrette, place the basil leaves, garlic, cheese, olive oil and lemon juice in a food processor. Season to taste with salt and pepper and process until the leaves are well chopped and the ingredients are combined. Alternatively, finely chop the basil leaves by hand and combine with the other vinaigrette ingredients. Pour the vinaigrette over the pasta and toss to coat.

Cut the tomatoes into wedges. Stone and halve the olives. Slice the sun-dried tomatoes. Toast the pine kernels on a baking tray under the hot grill until golden.

Add the tomatoes (fresh and sun-dried) and the olives to the pasta and mix until combined.

Transfer the pasta to a serving dish, sprinkle over the Parmesan and toasted pine kernels and serve garnished with a few basil leaves.

panzanella

serves 4–6

250 g/9 oz stale focaccia,
  ciabatta or French bread
4 large, vine-ripened
  tomatoes
about 6 tbsp extra-virgin
  olive oil
4 red, yellow and/or
  orange peppers
100 g/3½ oz cucumber
1 large red onion, finely
  chopped
8 canned anchovy fillets,
  drained and chopped
2 tbsp capers in brine,
  rinsed and patted dry
about 4 tbsp red wine
  vinegar
about 2 tbsp best-quality
  balsamic vinegar
salt and pepper
fresh basil leaves,
  to garnish

Cut the bread into 2.5-cm/1-inch cubes and place in a large bowl. Working over a plate to catch any juices, quarter the tomatoes; reserve the juices. Using a teaspoon, scoop out the cores and seeds and discard, then finely chop the flesh. Add to the bread cubes.

Drizzle 5 tablespoons of the olive oil over the mixture and toss with your hands until well coated. Pour in the reserved tomato juice and toss again. Set aside for about 30 minutes.

Meanwhile, cut the peppers in half and remove the cores and seeds. Place on a grill rack under a preheated hot grill and grill for 10 minutes, or until the skins are charred and the flesh softened. Place in a plastic bag, seal and set aside for 20 minutes to allow the steam to loosen the skins. Remove the skins, then finely chop.

Cut the cucumber in half lengthways, then cut each half into 3 strips lengthways. Using a teaspoon, scoop out and discard the seeds. Dice the cucumber.

Add the onion, peppers, cucumber, anchovy fillets and capers to the bread and toss together. Sprinkle with the red wine and balsamic vinegars and season to taste with salt and pepper. Drizzle with extra olive oil or vinegar if necessary, but be cautious that it does not become too greasy or soggy. Sprinkle the fresh basil leaves over the salad and serve at once.

a fresh salad with a zesty taste

spinach & orange
salad

∙∙

serves 4–6

225 g/8 oz baby spinach
   leaves
2 large oranges
½ red onion

dressing
3 tbsp extra-virgin olive oil
2 tbsp freshly squeezed
   orange juice
2 tsp lemon juice
1 tsp clear honey
½ tsp wholegrain mustard
salt and pepper

Wash the spinach leaves under cold running water and dry them thoroughly on kitchen paper. Remove and discard any tough stalks and tear the larger leaves into smaller pieces.

Slice the top and bottom off each orange with a sharp knife, then remove the peel. Carefully slice between the membranes of the orange to remove the segments.

Using a sharp knife, finely chop the onion. Mix the salad leaves and orange segments together and arrange in a serving dish. Scatter the chopped onion over the salad.

To make the dressing, whisk the olive oil, orange juice, lemon juice, honey, mustard and salt and pepper to taste together in a small bowl. Pour the dressing over the salad just before serving. Toss the salad well to coat the leaves with the dressing.

green bean & feta
salad

· ·

serves 4

350 g/12 oz green beans, trimmed
1 red onion, chopped
3–4 tbsp chopped fresh coriander
2 radishes, thinly sliced
75 g/2¾ oz feta cheese, crumbled
1 tsp chopped fresh oregano or ½ tsp dried oregano
pepper
2 tbsp red wine or fruit vinegar
5 tbsp extra-virgin olive oil
6 ripe cherry or small tomatoes, quartered

Bring about 5 cm/2 inches of water to the boil in the base of a steamer or in a medium saucepan. Add the green beans to the top of the steamer or place them in a metal colander set over the pan of water. Cover and steam for about 5 minutes until just tender.

Transfer the beans to a bowl and add the onion, coriander, radishes and feta cheese.

Sprinkle the oregano over the salad, then grind pepper over to taste. Whisk the vinegar and olive oil together and then pour over the salad. Toss gently to mix well.

Transfer to a serving platter, surround with the tomato quarters and serve at once or chill until ready to serve.

the perfect addition to any barbecue menu

potato salad

serves 4

700 g/1 lb 9 oz tiny new
  potatoes
8 spring onions
1 hard-boiled egg
  (optional)
250 ml/9 fl oz mayonnaise
1 tsp paprika
salt and pepper

to garnish
2 tbsp snipped fresh
  chives
pinch of paprika

Bring a large saucepan of lightly salted water to the boil. Add the potatoes and cook for 10–15 minutes, or until they are just tender.

Drain the potatoes and rinse them under cold running water until completely cold. Drain again. Transfer the potatoes to a bowl and reserve until required. Using a sharp knife, slice the spring onions thinly on the diagonal. Chop the hard-boiled egg, if using.

Mix the mayonnaise, paprika and salt and pepper to taste together in a bowl. Pour the mixture over the potatoes. Add the spring onions and egg, if using, to the potatoes and toss together.

Transfer the potato salad to a serving bowl, sprinkle with snipped chives and a pinch of paprika. Cover and leave to chill in the refrigerator until required.

coleslaw

serves 10–12

150 ml/5 fl oz mayonnaise
150 ml/5 fl oz low-fat
  natural yogurt
dash of Tabasco sauce
salt and pepper
1 medium head white
  cabbage
4 carrots
1 green pepper

To make the dressing, mix the mayonnaise, yogurt, Tabasco sauce and salt and pepper to taste together in a small bowl. Chill in the refrigerator until required.

Cut the cabbage in half and then into quarters. Remove and discard the tough centre stalk. Shred the cabbage leaves finely. Wash the leaves under cold running water and dry thoroughly on kitchen paper. Peel the carrots and shred in a food processor or on a mandolin. Alternatively, roughly grate the carrot. Quarter and deseed the pepper and cut the flesh into thin strips.

Mix the vegetables together in a large serving bowl and toss to mix. Pour over the dressing and toss until the vegetables are well coated. Cover and chill until required.

mayonnaise

**makes about 300 ml/
10 fl oz**

2 large egg yolks
2 tsp Dijon mustard
¾ tsp salt, or to taste
white pepper
2 tbsp lemon juice or white
   wine vinegar
about 300 ml/10 fl oz
   sunflower oil

Whizz the egg yolks with the Dijon mustard, salt and white pepper to taste in a food processor, blender or by hand. Add the lemon juice and whizz again.

With the motor still running or still beating, add the oil, drop by drop at first. When the sauce begins to thicken, the oil can then be added in a slow, steady stream. Taste and adjust the seasoning with extra salt, pepper and lemon juice if necessary. If the sauce seems too thick, slowly add 1 tablespoon hot water, single cream or lemon juice.

Use at once or store in an airtight container in the refrigerator for up to 1 week.

a garlic-infused variation on classic mayonnaise

aïoli

**makes about 225 ml/
8 fl oz**

3 large garlic cloves,
  finely chopped
2 egg yolks
225 ml/8 fl oz extra-virgin
  olive oil
1 tbsp lemon juice
1 tbsp lime juice
1 tbsp Dijon mustard
1 tbsp chopped fresh
  tarragon
salt and pepper
1 fresh tarragon sprig,
  to garnish

Ensure that all the ingredients are at room temperature. Place the garlic and egg yolks in a food processor and process until well blended. With the motor running, pour in the oil teaspoon by teaspoon through the feeder tube until the mixture starts to thicken, then pour in the remaining oil in a thin stream until a thick mayonnaise forms.

Add the lemon and lime juices, mustard and tarragon and season to taste with salt and pepper. Blend until smooth, then transfer to a non-metallic bowl. Garnish with a tarragon sprig. Cover with clingfilm and refrigerate until required.

this is a cool and fresh-tasting dip

cucumber &
yogurt dip

serves 4

1 small cucumber
300 ml/10 fl oz authentic
  Greek yogurt
1 large garlic clove,
  crushed
1 tbsp chopped fresh mint
  or dill
salt and pepper
warm pitta bread, to serve

Peel then coarsely grate the cucumber. Put in a sieve and squeeze out as much of the water as possible. Put the cucumber into a bowl.

Add the yogurt, garlic and chopped mint (reserve a little as a garnish, if liked) to the cucumber and season with pepper. Mix well together and chill in the fridge for about 2 hours before serving.

To serve, stir the cucumber and yogurt dip and transfer to a serving bowl. Sprinkle with salt and accompany with warmed pitta bread.

a well-loved, healthy and delicious dip

chickpea &
sesame dip

serves 8

225 g/8 oz chickpeas,
    covered with water and
    soaked overnight
juice of 2 large lemons
150 ml/¼ pint tahini paste
2 garlic cloves, crushed
4 tbsp extra-virgin olive oil
small pinch of ground
    cumin
salt and pepper
pitta bread, to serve

to garnish
1 tsp paprika
chopped flat-leaf parsley

Drain the chickpeas, put in a saucepan and cover with cold water. Bring to the boil then simmer for about 2 hours, until very tender.

Drain the chickpeas, reserving a little of the liquid, and put in a food processor, reserving a few to garnish. Blend the chickpeas until smooth, gradually adding the lemon juice and enough reserved liquid to form a smooth, thick purée. Add the tahini paste, garlic, 3 tablespoons of the olive oil and the cumin and blend until smooth. Season with salt and pepper.

Turn the mixture into a shallow serving dish and chill in the fridge for 2–3 hours before serving. To serve, mix the reserved olive oil with the paprika and drizzle over the top of the dish. Sprinkle with the parsley and the reserved chickpeas. Accompany with warm pitta bread.

a tangy dip full of vibrant summer flavours

guacamole

serves 4

2 large, ripe avocados
juice of 1 lime, or to taste
2 tsp olive oil
½ onion, finely chopped
1 fresh green chilli, such
   as poblano, deseeded and
   finely chopped
1 garlic clove, crushed
¼ tsp ground cumin
1 tbsp chopped fresh
   coriander
salt and pepper
tortilla chips, to serve
fresh dill or coriander
   sprigs, to garnish

Cut the avocados in half lengthways and twist the 2 halves in opposite directions to separate. Stab the stone with the point of a sharp knife and lift out.

Peel, then roughly chop the avocado halves and place in a non-metallic bowl. Squeeze over the lime juice and add the oil. Mash the avocados with a fork until the desired consistency is achieved – either chunky or smooth. Blend in the onion, chilli, garlic, cumin and chopped coriander, then season to taste with salt and pepper.

Transfer to a serving dish and serve immediately, to avoid discoloration, with tortilla chips and garnished with fresh dill sprigs.

this classic salsa is colourful and flavour-packed

tomato **salsa**

serves 6

450 g/1 lb firm,
   ripe tomatoes
1 fresh jalapeño or other
   small hot chilli pepper
2 tsp extra-virgin olive oil
1 garlic clove, crushed
grated rind and juice
   of 1 lime
pinch of sugar
4 tbsp chopped fresh
   coriander
salt
fresh coriander sprigs,
   to garnish

Using a sharp knife, finely dice the tomatoes and put into a bowl with the seeds. Halve the chilli, remove and discard the seeds and very finely dice the flesh. Add to the tomatoes.

Add all the remaining ingredients to the tomatoes, season to taste with salt and mix well together.

Turn the mixture into a small, non-metallic serving bowl, cover and leave at room temperature for 30 minutes to allow the flavours to combine. If not serving straight away, the salsa can be stored in the refrigerator for up to 2–3 days, but it is best if allowed to return to room temperature for 1 hour before serving. Serve garnished with fresh coriander sprigs.

a popular accompaniment to burgers and meats

grilled pepper relish

serves 6–8

1 each of yellow, red and
  green peppers
1 tbsp extra-virgin olive oil
½ tsp soft brown sugar
1 tsp balsamic vinegar
¼ tsp salt
¼ tsp paprika

Preheat the grill to medium. Put the peppers on to a grill rack and cook, turning frequently, for 15 minutes, or until the skins are charred all over.

Transfer the peppers to a bowl, immediately cover with a clean, damp tea towel and leave for at least 2 hours, or overnight, until cold.

When the peppers are cold, hold them over a clean bowl to collect the juices and peel off the skin. Remove and discard the stem, core and seeds and finely dice the flesh.

Add the diced peppers to the juices in the bowl, then add the oil, sugar, vinegar, salt and paprika. Stir together until well mixed and serve, or store in an airtight container in the refrigerator for up to 4–5 days.

home-made
tomato sauce

**makes about 500 ml/
18 fl oz**

1 tbsp butter
2 tbsp olive oil
1 onion, chopped
1 garlic clove, finely
  chopped
400 g/14 oz canned
  tomatoes or 450 g/1 lb
  fresh tomatoes, peeled
1 tbsp tomato purée
100 ml/3½ fl oz red wine
150 ml/5 fl oz vegetable
  stock
½ tsp sugar
1 bay leaf
salt and pepper

Melt the butter with the oil in a large saucepan over a medium heat, add the onion and garlic and cook, stirring frequently, for 5 minutes, or until the onion has softened and is beginning to brown.

Add all the remaining ingredients to the saucepan and season to taste with salt and pepper. Bring to the boil, then reduce the heat to low and leave to simmer, uncovered and stirring occasionally, for 30 minutes, or until the sauce has thickened.

Remove and discard the bay leaf, pour the sauce into a food processor or blender and process until smooth. Alternatively, using the back of a wooden spoon, push the sauce through a nylon sieve into a bowl.

If serving immediately, reheat the sauce gently in a pan. Alternatively, store and reheat before serving.

no barbecue meal would be complete without it

spicy bbq sauce

serves 4

2 tbsp sunflower oil
1 large onion, chopped
2 garlic cloves, chopped
225 g/8 oz canned chopped
  tomatoes
1 tbsp Worcestershire
  sauce
2 tbsp brown fruity sauce
2 tbsp light muscovado
  sugar
4 tbsp white wine vinegar
½ tsp mild chilli powder
¼ tsp mustard powder
dash of Tabasco sauce
salt and pepper
cooked sausages or burger
  in bread rolls, to serve.

Preheat the barbecue. To make the sauce, heat the oil in a saucepan and fry the onion and garlic for 4–5 minutes, until softened and just beginning to brown.

Add the tomatoes, Worcestershire sauce, brown fruity sauce, sugar, white wine vinegar, chilli powder, mustard powder and Tabasco sauce to the saucepan. Add salt and pepper to taste, and bring to the boil.

Reduce the heat and simmer gently for 10–15 minutes, until the sauce begins to thicken slightly, stirring occasionally. Set aside and keep warm until required.

Serve with cooked sausages or burgers.

Desserts & Drinks

toffee fruit kebabs

serves 4

2 dessert apples, cored and
cut into wedges
2 firm pears, cored and
cut into wedges
juice of ½ lemon
25 g/1 oz light muscovado
sugar
¼ tsp ground allspice
25 g/1 oz unsalted butter,
melted

sauce

125 g/4½ oz butter
100 g/3½ oz light
muscovado sugar
6 tbsp double cream

Preheat the barbecue. Toss the apples and pears in the lemon
juice to prevent any discoloration.

Mix the sugar and allspice together and sprinkle over the fruit.
Thread the fruit pieces on to skewers.

To make the toffee sauce, place the butter and sugar in a
saucepan and heat, stirring gently, until the butter has melted
and the sugar has dissolved.

Add the cream to the saucepan and bring to the boil. Boil for
1–2 minutes, then leave to cool slightly.

Meanwhile, place the fruit kebabs over hot coals and cook for
5 minutes, turning and basting frequently with the melted butter,
until the fruit is just tender. Transfer the fruit kebabs to warmed
serving plates and serve with the cooled toffee sauce.

bananas lend themselves perfectly
to barbecuing

chocolate rum bananas

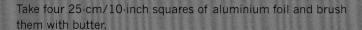

serves 4

1 tbsp butter
225 g/8 oz plain or milk
   chocolate
4 large bananas
2 tbsp rum
crème fraîche, mascarpone
   cheese or ice cream,
   to serve
grated nutmeg,
   to decorate

Take four 25-cm/10-inch squares of aluminium foil and brush them with butter.

Grate the chocolate. Make a careful slit lengthways in the peel of each banana, and open just wide enough to insert the chocolate. Place the grated chocolate inside the bananas, along their lengths, then close them up.

Wrap each stuffed banana in a square of foil, then barbecue them over hot coals for about 5–10 minutes, or until the chocolate has melted inside the bananas. Remove from the barbecue, place the bananas on individual serving plates and pour some rum into each banana.

Serve at once with crème fraîche, mascarpone cheese or ice cream, topped with nutmeg.

mascarpone
peaches

- -

serves 4

4 peaches
175 g/6 oz mascarpone
  cheese
40 g/1½ oz pecan nuts or
  walnuts, chopped
1 tsp sunflower oil
4 tbsp maple syrup

Cut the peaches in half and remove the stones. If you are preparing this recipe in advance, press the peach halves together and wrap in clingfilm until required.

Mix the mascarpone cheese and pecans together in a bowl until well combined. Leave to chill in the refrigerator until required. Preheat the barbecue. Brush the peach halves with a little sunflower oil and place on a rack set over medium hot coals. Cook the peach halves for 5–10 minutes, turning once, until hot.

Transfer the peach halves to a serving dish and top with the mascarpone and nut mixture. Drizzle the maple syrup over the peaches and mascarpone filling and serve immediately.

fresh pineapple and rum are a magical combination

totally tropical
pineapple

• •

serves 4

1 pineapple
3 tbsp dark rum
2 tbsp muscovado sugar
1 tsp ground ginger
4 tbsp unsalted butter,
  melted

Preheat the barbecue. Using a sharp knife, cut off the crown of the pineapple, then cut the fruit into 2-cm/¾-inch thick slices. Cut away the peel from each slice and flick out the 'eyes' with the point of the knife. Stamp out the cores with an apple corer or small pastry cutter.

Mix the rum, sugar, ginger and butter together in a jug, stirring constantly, until the sugar has dissolved. Brush the pineapple rings with the rum mixture.

Cook the pineapple rings over hot coals for 3–4 minutes on each side. Transfer to serving plates and serve immediately with the remaining rum mixture poured over them.

succulent figs with melting cheese and cinnamon

stuffed figs

● ●

serves 4

8 fresh figs
100 g/3½ oz cream cheese
1 tsp powdered cinnamon
3 tbsp brown sugar
natural yogurt, crème
   fraîche, mascarpone
   cheese or ice cream,
   to serve

Cut out eight 18-cm/7-inch squares of aluminium foil. Make a small slit in each fig, then place each fig on a square of foil.

Put the cream cheese in a bowl. Add the cinnamon and stir until well combined. Stuff the inside of each fig with the cinnamon cream cheese, then sprinkle a teaspoon of sugar over each one. Close the foil round each fig to make a parcel.

Place the parcels on the barbecue and cook over hot coals, turning them frequently, for about 10 minutes, or until the figs are cooked to your taste.

Transfer the figs to serving plates and serve at once with natural yogurt, crème fraîche, mascarpone cheese or ice cream.

a delicious treat to end any barbecued meal

panettone with mascarpone &
strawberries

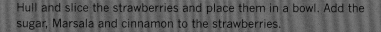

serves 4

225 g/8 oz strawberries
25 g/1 oz caster sugar
6 tbsp Marsala wine
½ tsp ground cinnamon
4 slices panettone
4 tbsp mascarpone cheese

Hull and slice the strawberries and place them in a bowl. Add the sugar, Marsala and cinnamon to the strawberries.

Toss the strawberries in the sugar and cinnamon mixture until they are well coated. Leave to chill in the refrigerator for at least 30 minutes.Preheat the barbecue. When ready to serve, transfer the slices of panettone to a rack set over medium hot coals. Cook the panettone for 1 minute on each side, or until golden brown.

Remove the panettone from the barbecue and transfer to serving plates. Top the panettone with the mascarpone cheese and the marinated strawberries. Serve immediately.

tasty fruit chunks in a honey-liqueur sauce

mixed **fruit kebabs**

• •

serves 4

2 nectarines, halved and
   stoned
2 kiwi fruit
4 red plums
1 mango, peeled, halved
   and stoned
2 bananas, peeled and
   thickly sliced
8 strawberries, hulled
1 tbsp clear honey
3 tbsp Cointreau

Cut the nectarine halves into wedges and place in a large, shallow dish. Peel and quarter the kiwi fruit. Cut the plums in half and remove the stones. Cut the mango flesh into chunks and add to the dish with the kiwi fruit, plums, bananas and strawberries.

Mix the honey and Cointreau together in a jug until well blended. Pour the mixture over the fruit and toss lightly to coat. Cover with clingfilm and leave to marinate in the refrigerator for 1 hour.

Preheat the barbecue. Drain the fruit, reserving the marinade. Thread the fruit on to several presoaked wooden skewers and cook over medium hot coals, turning and brushing frequently with the reserved marinade, for 5–7 minutes, then serve.

this well-loved cooler is a traditional favourite

fresh lemonade

makes 1.2 litres/2 pints

4 large lemons, preferably
  unwaxed or organic
175 g/6 oz caster sugar
850 ml/1½ pints boiling
  water
ice cubes, to serve

Scrub the lemons well and dry. Using a vegetable peeler, peel 3 of the lemons very thinly. Place the peel in a large jug or basin, add the sugar and boiling water and stir well until the sugar has dissolved. Cover the jug and leave to stand for at least 3 hours, stirring occasionally. Meanwhile, squeeze the juice from the 3 lemons and reserve.

Strain the lemon peel and stir in the reserved lemon juice. Thinly slice the remaining lemon and cut the slices in half. Add to the lemonade together with the ice cubes. Stir and serve.

a non-alcoholic version of the classic
Spanish drink

^{soft} sangria

· ·

makes 2 litres/3½ pints

1.5 litres/2¾ pints red
   grape juice
300 ml/10 fl oz orange
   juice
75 ml/2½ fl oz cranberry
   juice
50 ml/1¾ fl oz lemon juice
50 ml/1¾ fl oz lime juice
100 ml/3½ fl oz sugar
   syrup
ice cubes

to decorate
slices of lemon
slices of orange
slices of lime

Put the grape juice, orange juice, cranberry juice, lemon juice,
lime juice and sugar syrup into a chilled punch bowl and stir well.

Add the ice and decorate with the slices of lemon, orange
and lime.

*the ideal refresher on a hot
summer's day*

orange & lime
iced tea

• •

serves 2

300 ml/10 fl oz water
2 tea bags
100 ml/3½ fl oz orange
   juice
4 tbsp lime juice
1–2 tbsp brown sugar
8 ice cubes

to decorate
wedge of lime
granulated sugar
slices of fresh orange,
   lemon or lime

Pour the water into a saucepan and bring to the boil.
Remove from the heat, add the tea bags and leave to infuse for
5 minutes. Remove the tea bags and leave the tea to cool to room
temperature (about 30 minutes). Transfer to a jug, cover with
clingfilm and chill in the refrigerator for at least 45 minutes.

When the tea has chilled, pour in the orange juice and lime juice.
Add sugar to taste.

Take two glasses and rub the rims with a wedge of lime, then
dip them in granulated sugar to frost. Put the ice cubes into
the glasses and pour over the tea. Decorate with slices of fresh
orange, lemon or lime and serve.

an irresistibly attractive adult-only tipple

singapore sling

· ·

serves 1

10–12 cracked ice cubes
2 measures gin
1 measure cherry brandy
1 measure lemon juice
1 tsp grenadine
soda water, to top up

to decorate
lime peel
cocktail cherries

Put 4–6 cracked ice cubes into a cocktail shaker. Pour the gin, cherry brandy, lemon juice and grenadine over the ice. Shake vigorously until a frost forms.

Half fill a chilled highball glass with cracked ice cubes and strain the cocktail over them. Top up with soda water and decorate with lime peel and cocktail cherries.

a classic combination of tequila, triple sec and lime

margarita

serves 1

lime wedge
coarse salt
4–6 cracked ice cubes
3 measures white tequila
1 measure triple sec
2 measures lime juice
slice of lime, to decorate

Rub the rim of a chilled cocktail glass with the lime wedge and then dip in a saucer of coarse salt to frost.

Put the cracked ice cubes into a cocktail shaker. Pour the tequila, triple sec and lime juice over the ice. Shake vigorously until a frost forms.

Strain into the prepared glass and decorate with the lime slice.

a cooling and refreshing drink with a kick

club mojito

• •

serves 1

1 tsp syrup de gomme
a few fresh mint leaves
juice of ½ lime
ice cubes
2 measures Jamaican rum
soda water, to top up
dash Angostura bitters

Put the syrup, mint leaves and lime juice in a highball glass and crush or muddle the mint leaves.

Add ice and rum, then top up with soda water to taste.

Finish with a dash of Angostura bitters.

index